JOHN KEATS

CRITICAL ISSUES

Published

Jane Austen	*Darryl Jones*
George Eliot	*Pauline Nestor*
Virginia Woolf	*Linden Peach*
Charlotte Brontë	*Carl Plasa*
Charles Dickens	*Lyn Pykett*
Henry James	*Jeremy Tambling*
John Keats	*John Whale*
William Wordsworth	*John Williams*

In preparation

Geoffrey Chaucer	*Ruth Evans*
James Joyce	*Kiernan Ryan*
D. H. Lawrence	*Rick Rylance*
Joseph Conrad	*Allan Simmons*
Thomas Hardy	*Julian Wolfreys*

Critical Issues Series
Series Standing Order
ISBN 1–4039–2158–X hardcover
ISBN 1–4039–2159–8 paperback
(*outside North America only*)

You can receive future titles in this series as they are published by placing a standing order. Please contact your bookseller or, in case of difficulty, write to us at the address below with your name and address, the title of the series and the ISBN quoted above.

Customer Services Department, Macmillan Distribution Ltd
Houndmills, Basingstoke, Hampshire RG21 6XS, England

Critical Issues

John Keats

John Whale

First published 2005 by
PALGRAVE MACMILLAN
Houndmills, Basingstoke, Hampshire RG21 6XS and
175 Fifth Avenue, New York, N.Y. 10010
Companies and representatives throughout the world.

PALGRAVE MACMILLAN is the global academic imprint of the Palgrave Macmillan division of St. Martin's Press, LLC and of Palgrave Macmillan Ltd. Macmillan® is a registered trademark in the United States, United Kingdom and other countries. Palgrave is a registered trademark in the European Union and other countries.

ISBN 0–333–99448–5 hardback
ISBN 0–333–99449–3 paperback

This book is printed on paper suitable for recycling and made from fully managed and sustained forest sources.

A catalogue record for this book is available from the British Library.

A catalog record for this book is available from the Library of Congress

For
Helen Whale and Lucy Whale

Contents

Acknowledgements

Thanks are due to the Faculty of Arts and to the School of English here in the University of Leeds for granting me the leave in which to write this book. The School of English continues to be an extremely supportive environment in which to work, not least because of the generosity of friends and colleagues. David Fairer was generous in sharing his knowledge of how poems work and Vivien Jones, as ever, offered me her time and her shrewd critical intelligence. Martin Coyle took up where he left off in 1983, this time offering his encouragement and practical good sense in the guise of series editor. At home, I'm grateful for support from Sally, Helen, and Lucy. This study of early nineteenth-century masculinity is dedicated to two young twenty-first-century women: my daughters.

Preface

There has always been a great temptation to read Keats's poetry biographically, and it's true that the tragic and painful circumstances of his illness and early death are part of the experience that went to make the poems. This study approaches Keats's poetry through the perspective of sexuality and gender identity. It parallels the poet's experience as a relatively young man in early nineteenth-century England, but it does so without using biography as the pre-eminent authority with which to determine or explain the significance of the poems. My main concern is always for the poems themselves and their creative exploration of sexuality, romance, and the nature of masculine identity for an ambitious and talented young poet. Keats's letters are indicative here. While they are extremely helpful in identifying the ways in which Keats explores the connections between poetry, romance, and sexuality, they are also texts in their own right, constituting an extraordinarily distinctive form of writing in which his creativity examines the self and the often conflicting demands of passion and literary ambition.

This study returns to the scene of identity and sexuality in order to understand the major part that these play in the poems: this is their subject, not simply the background from which they were produced. What I hope emerges from this return to the subject of Keats and gendered identity is a different attention to the poems. Recent criticism has in the main been intensely focused on the political aspect of Keats's poetry. The earlier view of Keats as a largely apolitical and feminine writer, aestheticised in the way he was first promoted by the Victorians, has been largely exorcised. Many of the most powerful and subtle readings of the odes in the last fifteen years, for example, have been concerned to explore the political affiliation or the political matrix of the poems. To return to the question of identity and the role of the poet can complement the effect of this relatively recent wave of historicist reassessment. As Jeffrey Cox has demonstrated in his work on the Cockney school, sexuality and political identity go hand in hand for Keats and many of his contemporaries.

What I hope emerges from the following pages is a fresh and lively reassessment of Keats's poetry which captures the urgency and complexity of his engagement with the competing demands of self and sexuality alongside his self-confirmed vocation as a poet. At times, this attention to the libidinous energy of Keats's texts may have the effect of presenting him in a seemingly negative light. Forms of aggressive heterosexual desire and the obvious, self-proclaimed difficulty of coming to terms with women form the disconcerting subject of many of the poems. Some allowance must be made here for Keats's youthfulness and some respect paid to the historical difference of the time and social class which produced his gendered identity. There's a laudable, sometimes searing, honesty in the letters on such matters. But it's not Keats's morality or ethical standing which lies at the forefront of my concerns here. Even at its most unattractive to twenty-first-century liberal mores, Keats's response to his own sexuality and its complex involvement with his poetic aspirations remains compelling and, perhaps most importantly, highly creative. For all the anguish and conflict registered in his explorations of passion, it's his creativity which matters.

All references to Keats's poems are to *John Keats: the Complete Poems*, edited by John Barnard (Penguin: Harmondsworth, 2nd edn, 1976), hereafter cited as *Poems*. References to Keats's letters, hereafter cited as *Letters*, are to: *The Letters of John Keats 1814–1821*, 2 vols. Edited by Hyder Edward Rollins (Harvard University Press: Cambridge MA, 1958). Please note: this text does not regularise Keats's inconsistent, non-standard and often creative spelling.

1

'Modern Love'

I. KEATS AND THE FEMININE

John Keats has been more readily associated with the 'feminine' than any other canonical male English poet.[1] Recent critics, Victorian editors and literary historians, as well as his own contemporaries – including his friends and literary opponents – have all shown a readiness to place him within this culturally defined category. Keats's 'feminisation' was always likely, given his tragically early death and the mythologising which took place soon after. The now discredited, but long-standing idea that he had been killed by the reviews, coupled with the effect produced by his acquaintance Percy Shelley's pastoral elegy 'Adonais' dedicated to Keats, conspired to produce, as they would for Shelley himself not long afterwards, a compelling story of poetic martyrdom involving the sacrifice of a sensitive soul somehow unfitted for the world. The cult of biography which attached itself to Keats by the mid-nineteenth century could even use his physical appearance in the form of his death-masks and portraits to construct an image of the sensitive 'feminine' poet whose status as a man was marginal by conventional standards. Beyond such biographical mythologising, the category of the 'feminine', however, is also one which has frequently and complexly intersected his writings and his reception through different historical audiences.

The role played by the feminine alongside other issues of gender and sexuality in Keats's more famous poems is the subject of subsequent chapters. In order to understand these issues, however, it is first necessary to locate some of the main impulses in his writing and to provide a context to show how Keats's famous poetic articulations of a passionate intensity and his exploration of an

empathetic form of imagination emerge from a complex engagement with the social conventions of his time, the celebration of
friendship with other men, and the difficulty of his relationship
with women. Keats's involvement with a coterie of friends can be
seen to be extremely instrumental in his development as a poet and,
alongside that, in his development of the idea of a poetic selfhood.
As we shall see in a number of fascinating, sometimes disturbing, examples from his letters, Keats's progression as a poet is
matched by his own very playful – and at the same time rigorous –
exploration of selfhood.

One of the main tensions in Keats's writing, whether in verse or
prose, is provided by his attraction towards the abstracted or mythical and his passionate engagement with the particularity of his
own time. At its best, Keats's work combines, on the one hand, a
sensuous appreciation of the body and its sexual experiences, and,
on the other, a desire for a spiritualised transcendence. His 'Ode to
a Nightingale', for example, famously moves within the space of a
single line from a 'high requiem' to a 'sod', demonstrating how his
poetry can successfully offer a sensuous appreciation of the real,
yet yearn for the exalted heights available in the impersonal realm
of art. The purpose of this opening chapter is, then, to explore
Keats's conscientious struggle to mediate between his contemporaneity and the transhistorical or eternal by reference to some of his
lesser known poems, his anxious letters on the subject of women,
and the subject of fashion. From these examples, a less familiar
Keats emerges: a poet in some ways passionately at odds with his
society and his class position within it, but whose immediate circle
of friends, family and acquaintances can also provide the inspiration for a broad variety of inventive poems.

By engaging with Keats in the context of his own milieu, it is also
possible to form a more precise and historically inflected definition
of the way in which the issues of gender and sexuality inform his
poetry. These issues were something with which Keats was both
anxiously and creatively engaged. As a young man and as a developing poet, they were central to his sense of identity. In what follows, Keats is seen to engage in a fraught articulation of his
relationship to both gender and sexuality. In that regard, he shares
in the difficulty experienced by many young men in his own lower-
middle-class position in early nineteenth-century British society.
Much more extraordinary, however, on the basis of his surviving
letters, is the way in which he could explore that difficult territory

with friends and at the same time make it a central facet of his creative work as a poet.

The 'feminine' is a category which Keats himself uses to describe one of the states of mind conducive to creativity and one which helps him define the otherwise strange 'labour' of the poet in relation to other forms of work which themselves are conventionally seen in socially gendered terms. For his contemporaries, including the essayist William Hazlitt and the poet Lord Byron, the feminine was a category which they, too, used to define their own different forms of masculinity. It was also a term which figured at the centre of critical disputes within the highly charged and politicised review culture of the time. In these often vitriolic arguments the representation of sexuality within literary forms such as poetry was an extremely contentious issue, one riven with both political and class antagonisms.

In the following letter, dated 19 March 1819, Keats himself deploys the idea of 'effeminacy' with a good deal of self-consciousness and with a startling degree of physiological precision:

> This morning I am in a sort of temper indolent and supremely careless:
> I long after a stanza or two of Thompson's Castle of indolence – My
> passions are all alseep from my having slumbered till nearly eleven
> and weakened the animal fibre all over me to a delightful sensation
> about three degrees on this side of faintness – if I had teeth of pearl
> and the breath of lillies I should call it langour – but as I am * I must
> call it Laziness – In this state of effeminacy the fibres of the brain are
> relaxed in common with the rest of the body, and to such a happy
> degree that pleasure has no show of enticement and [...] pain no
> unbearable frown. Neither Poetry, nor Ambition, nor Love have any
> alertness of countenance as they pass by me: they seem rather like
> three figures on a greek vase – a Man and two women – whom no one
> but myself could distinguish in their disguisement. This is the only
> happiness; and is a rare instance of advantage in the body overpow-
> ering the Mind. (Letters, II, 78–9)[2]

This prose description provides the real-life backdrop for Keats's 'Ode on Indolence', but it is one mediated by gender and aesthetics as Keats reaches after the right word to describe the experience – 'indolence', 'langour', 'laziness' – and draws on the poetic authority of James Thomson's Castle of Indolence (1748) behind it; 'langour', as the allusion to 'teeth of pearl and the breath of lillies' indicates, is connected to his idea of woman's experience and identity; 'laziness', in this context, brings him back to an awareness of his determinedly male sense of achievement as a poet. Despite all these somewhat inadequate categorisations, the passage develops its definition and exploration of a state of consciousness which challenges – and reverses – conventional ideas of achievement and the ethics of work, even if, as here, that work consists of the operation of a poet's fancy. Keats pushes at the limits of consciousness and is seemingly delighted at the liberation afforded by the body's 'overpowering the Mind'. In celebrating the creative potential of sleeping 'till nearly eleven', he is, of course, in danger of justifying one of the most familiar traits of adolescence. More pertinently for our study, he demonstrates what has come to be seen as one of his most valuable and creative characteristics: the ability to revel in and enjoy the loss of those aspects of self which are often celebrated within our culture because of the confirmation of identity which they provide. Here the softness of the body and the brain, as well as the consequent loss of the mind's rational autonomy, stand in defiance of mainstream philosophical and moral thought. Keats luxuriates not only in the freedom from rational autonomy, but also from the business of pleasure and pain.

If 'effeminacy' was a category which Keats invoked to explore the character and limits of his own creative states of mind, it was also used in a much more pejorative way by his contemporaries. William Hazlitt included a consideration of his friend John Keats in his essay 'On the Effeminacy of Character', published in the second volume of his *Table Talk* in 1822.[3] Though Hazlitt was some seventeen years older, the two men shared many aesthetic ideas and had a good deal in common. They were both members of an aspirant lower middle class and both sought for distinction within the realm of polite letters. Both men demonstrate a similarly robust, corporeal masculinity attracted to sporting activities such as boxing while being aggressively disposed towards aristocratic sophistication and dandyism. Both combine their literary intelligence, commitment and learning with a need to retain their rank-based suspicion of aristocratic over-refinement and display. This conflicted combination inflects the whole of Hazlitt's essay on effeminacy which is typically comparative – always posing opposites against each other in its forceful search for definition. Hazlitt begins with an explanation of 'effeminacy of character' based on sensibility: 'Effeminacy of character arises from a prevalence of the sensibility over the will.' Effeminacy of character, for Hazlitt, is synonymous with cultural refinement, over-sophistication and ease. It lacks the urgency brought about by an awareness of life's vicissitudes such as 'pain, or labour, or danger, or death'. In terms of time and self, it is characterised by a selfish, almost childish, living in and for the moment.

Posed against such an effete, complacent and potentially immoral character, Hazlitt offers what appears to be the preferred figure of his own manliness: 'There is nothing more to be esteemed than a manly firmness and decision of character.' In keeping with the muscularity of his own hard-hitting prose, he professes to like 'a person who knows his own mind and sticks to it; who sees at once what is to be done in given circumstances and does it'. Hazlitt the committed radical here declaims against the false luxuriousness of a Hamlet-like dallying and procrastination. Towards its end, the essay plays off an attraction towards the 'vulgar and violent, harsh and repulsive' against the 'softness and smoothness' of those who demonstrate effeminacy of character. In so doing, it begins to expose the social tensions underlying its gendered definition of character and writing: the clash between cultural refinement and vulgarity.

As he begins his consideration of Keats's poetry Hazlitt shifts the ground from effeminacy of character to an effeminacy of style: 'By an effeminate style,' he explains, 'I would be understood to mean one that is florid, all fine; that cloys by its sweetness, and tires by its sameness.' Byron is excluded from the category, despite Hazlitt's hostile recognition of his social origins: 'Lord Byron is a pampered and aristocratic writer, but he is not effeminate.' His friend Keats, on the other hand, seems to him to have had a 'fault' which consisted of 'a deficiency in masculine energy of style'. Hazlitt sees 'tenderness' and 'delicacy' evident in Keats's poems to 'an uncommon degree', but notes that there is a want of 'strength and substance'. *Endymion* is clearly symptomatic of this 'deficiency'; it is the product of a 'youthful imagination'.[4] Hazlitt's critique of Keats here seems overly influenced by the latter's recent death. Early death seems to suggest to Hazlitt a stress on Keats's immaturity in which the poet's 'effeminacy' is seen not simply as feminine, but as boyish or adolescent: masculinity not yet confirmed and developed into its matured manliness. Hazlitt makes a typically gendered distinction between imagination and the fancy, but then goes on to a much more corporeal and strongly defined notion of masculinity: 'All is soft and fleshy, without bone or muscle. We see in him the youth, without the manhood of poetry.' Once again, Hazlitt defines Keats's effeminacy of style by comparing it with a masculinity metaphorically represented by the strong, mature and healthy male body. Effeminacy, in this context, is concerned with the differences between refined forms of culture and notions of vulgarity – with what diminishes an implied standard of esteemed masculinity. To that extent, it is more intent on presenting Keats as 'youthful' than as 'feminine' – not quite yet a man, rather than standing in opposition to man.

If Hazlitt's account of Keats's 'effeminacy of style' is concerned to retain a strong sense of the lost potential of his recently deceased friend and to refrain from the claim that he also suffered from an 'effeminacy of character', there is no such restraint in Byron's response to Keats's poetry. His focus is much more explicitly and confidently directed at the link between Keats's poetry and its representation of sexuality. In part, this is because most of the comments are delivered in the relatively private context of conversation or correspondence between friends and associates, not in the public domain of print. In these fascinating responses, it could be said that Byron confidently deploys the discourse of sexuality in order to expose what he sees as the inadequacies of Keats's poetry. For example, in an often-quoted letter to the publisher John Murray, he refers to the 'trash' of 'Johnny Keats's *p-ss a bed* poetry', and, after calling on the publishing world to 'flay him alive', complains that he cannot bear 'the drivelling idiotism of the Mankin'.[5] Byron seems intent on diminishing and infantilising Keats here, both in the reference to 'Johnny' and by describing him as a 'mankin', by which one assumes he means literally a 'little man'. Whatever Byron's precise intention, the effect is to represent Keats as a kind of idiot boy: someone from whom he wishes, at least, to withhold the full status of a man. In another letter to Murray, written only weeks later in September 1820, Byron extends his attack on Keats with a particularly graphic anecdote from the realm of prostitution:

> [...] his is the * of Poetry – something like the pleasure an Italian fid-dler extracted out of being suspended daily by a Street Walker in Drury Lane. This went on for some weeks: at last the Girl went to get a pint of Gin – met another, chatted too long, and Cornelli was *hanged out-right before she returned.* Such like is the trash they praise, and such will be the end of the *outstretched* poesy of this miserable Self-polluter of the human mind.[6]

Whereas in the earlier letter Keats was compared with an incontinent boy in order to indicate his lack of manliness, he is now castigated as a masturbator – even in our present society, a familiar form of abuse when groups of men challenge each other. To be accused of being a masturbator in this context, presumably, is to impugn the other man's sexual capability or potency. Not content with this, Byron takes the point even further, as if to demonstrate Keats's own push towards excess by referring his correspondent to the case of the Italian fiddler. This, in its turn, seems to confirm the perverse desire to pleasure oneself in something other than heterosexual penetrative sex even when that commodity is immediately available. There's an interesting mixture of assumed confidence and fascination in Byron's bravura man-of-the-world doing down of Keats here. His references to street-walkers and Drury Lane reveal a willingness to conceive of poetry in terms of the sexual analogy and they contain a strong condemnation of the vulgar commodification of literature:

> such writing is a sort of mental masturbation – ********* his *Imagination*. I don't mean he is *indecent*, but viciously soliciting his own ideas into a state, which is neither poetry nor any thing else but a Bedlam vision produced by raw pork and opium.[7]

Like Hazlitt, Byron homes in on the seemingly excessive artifice of Keats's poetry which is linked to an adolescent or unformed sexuality which he sees as immoral or perverse. Byron's account, unlike Hazlitt's, is however, also ruthlessly underscored by its sense of superior social rank which mocks at the way in which this lower-middle-class writer explores sexuality through romance. In so doing, Byron's graphic attacks set the agenda for many future accounts of the link between sexuality and social class in Keats's poetry.

In general, recent criticism has followed Byron and Hazlitt and understood both Keats's distinctive kind of creativity and his position within culture as 'feminine'. His celebration of states of mind or consciousness in which the self appears to be lost, absorbed, or mobile clearly questions dominant assumptions and conventions about the nature of identity and the power, autonomy and authority of the self. Since the self in this dominant form is also assumed in culture to be empowered, it is read as masculine. Challenging it or simply standing outside these paradigms is thus deemed to be 'feminine'. Margaret Homans, reflecting cautiously on this kind of configuration, puts it fairly starkly: 'if gender is a social construct, and if to be socially powerless is to be "a woman", then Keats can be classed among women.'[8] In his letters, as we shall see, Keats is intent on exploring and arguing for a kind of selfhood which rejects the conventional, ego-based identity that prizes confirmed individuality as well as the dominance of rational self-consciousness and the exercise of the will. Through these extraordinary texts he begins to define a new form of selfhood in keeping with the kind of artist he finds himself to be. The most celebrated of these explorations value the loss of identity as a means of encountering the nature of others, whether people or things; and they indicate a deep-seated reaction against the certainty of selfhood even if it leads to the impressive literary creations of a Wordsworth or a Milton.

Keats's attacks on egotistical, dogmatic and fixed forms of identity and artwork are, of course, relatively easy to identify with from a liberal perspective. They are more unsettling and radical when, as so often with Keats, they are attached to a profound belief in the self as a process rather than fixed or established, to a championing of the capacity to live with uncertainty and, perhaps most problematic of all, to a relish for what seems like an anti-intellectual urge to move beyond or outside rational self-consciousness. Within this unsystematic, but persistent and highly self-conscious set of reflections, Keats arrives at ideas such as 'the cameleon poet' and 'Negative Capability' which have, ironically, subsequently been used by critics as a means of establishing a Keatsian aesthetic of identity through which the poems can be read.

On the basis of such daring speculative enquiries into the peculiar nature of the poet Anne K. Mellor argues that 'Keats's poetic theory is self-consciously positioned within the realm of the feminine gender'. 'A self that continually overflows itself, that melts into the Other, that *becomes* the Other,' she argues, 'is conventionally associated with the female.' Both Homans and Mellor reveal their concern at the ease with which Keats can be admitted to the category: 'Keats *can* be classed' [my italics] and 'is conventionally associated with' indicate some of their underlying qualms about placing Keats within the 'feminine', even if in the case of Mellor this takes the form of transferring the anxiety onto the poet: 'Occupying the position of a woman in the poetic discourse of the early nineteenth century was however a source of anxiety for

Keats.'[9] The over-confidence with which Keats has sometimes been said to occupy woman's position is explored in Philip Cox's shrewd analysis of genre in relation to his supposed 'effeminacy'.[10] And as we have already seen in the examples from Hazlitt and Byron, placing Keats in the category of the feminine often tells us more about competing forms of masculinity than it does about the position of woman.

With this in mind, other critics have concentrated their attention on the ways in which Keats's experimentation with language and poetic form redefines him in relation to the boundaries of the usual masculine domain. Marlon B. Ross acknowledges Keats's exploration of 'nonpatrilinear' uses of language and sees this as a 'refusal of patriarchal power' which has negative implications for Keats's aesthetic.[11] Given its deliberate distancing of itself from power, he asks how it can still possess the power necessary to change the culture. What Ross perceives as the dilemma of Keats's linguistic experimentation leads him to invoke a very differently positioned, but equally gendered term. In such a situation, according to Ross, Keats 'is immediately perceived, and perceives himself, as impotent'. According to this scenario, Keats's transgressive avant-gardism leads him outside the masculine mainstream, but is still defined by its confirmedly gendered, and dis-empowered characteristics.

In 'Feminizing Keats',[12] Susan J. Wolfson observes how Keats's gender has always been an issue, and she reflects intelligently on the way in which his reception in his own time, later in the Victorian period, and within more recent feminist criticism, is characterised by an insistence on his marginality in terms of masculinity and is structured along the following lines:

> [...] he either triggers efforts to stabilize and enforce standards of manly conduct in which he is the negative example, stigmatized as 'effeminate', or 'unmanly'; or he inspires attempts to broaden and make more flexible prevailing definitions so that certain qualities, previously limited to and sometimes derided as 'feminine', may be allowed to enrich and enlarge the culture's images of 'manliness' – even to the point of androgyny.[13]

Looking at Victorian responses, Wolfson particularly focuses on the extent to which Keats is invoked in order to construct a standard of manliness and to regulate this manliness by the inclusion of a feminine aspect within it. Quoting the late nineteenth-century novelist Margaret Oliphant – '[i]n poetry his was the women's part' – Wolfson extends the issue of Keats and gender beyond a mere 'default from the code of manliness' to include qualities with a 'particular appeal to women'.[14]

Keats's youthful, sometimes gauche, explorations of romance and sexuality have also been examined in relation to his lower-middle-class background. Social class and masculinity are here joined together in a manner which mirrors Byron's famous attacks. Taking her lead from these, Marjorie Levinson offers a socio-sexual reading of Keats's poetry which sees its 'style' as symptomatic of what she terms 'the petty bourgeoisie'.[15] In this style she identifies a 'dream of masturbation', a fantasy she locates in the exhibitionist self-fashioning of the middle class. She thus presents Keats's production of an excessive, overwrought style as characteristic of his social class's self-promotion and self-alienation. The figure of masturbation, according to Levinson's thesis, is, paradoxically, richly creative, enabling Keats to produce a form of poetry marked by excess: a style which operates like a translation or parody of previous poetry.[16] Levinson's is one of the more extravagant of recent estimates of Keats's work and can easily be seen as lacking in historical specificity, but her work is strongly embedded in Keats criticism: both the negative criticism of his own time and in more recent accounts, most notably Christopher Ricks's influential study of Keats and embarrassment[17] which established the richness of his poetry in his self-conscious play on various forms of awkwardness. In this respect, Ricks extends the cerebral study of paradox which was such a significant feature of Keats criticism in the middle of the twentieth century with the so-called New Critics into a more physiological and experiential form of ambiguity.

After a brief period in which feminist criticism might be said to have experimented with the feminine potential of Keats's 'negative capability' the balance now seems to have turned in favour of addressing the competing masculine and feminine forces within Keats's make-up as a poet. To this end, Alan Bewell focuses on the problem of Keats's own shift of style between, on the one hand, the earlier poetry and, on the other, *Hyperion* and the famous odes. He challenges and explores the long-held view that 'a passive, weak, poetry of sensual excess – viewed as "effeminate" by Keats's contemporaries' – is 'displaced by a more serious, more masculine, philosophical poetry that seeks to master literary traditions'.[18] The 'fundamental, unresolved conflict of Keats's later verse', he argues, 'lies in his struggle, often against his own better poetic instincts, to distance himself from the intimacy with women and women's floral style that he sought in his earlier poems'. For Bewell, Keats displays 'an increasing recognition and discomfort with contemporary attitudes toward gender and with the ways in which the age demanded an author's gender be expressed in a specific style'.[19] More recently and more generally, Daniel P. Watkins has identified a 'sadeian logic' at work in Keats's poetry. He sees the poetry as part of a larger historical configuration of self, sexuality and authority which turns the poet's insertion in the classical realm of love – best illustrated in the 'Ode to Psyche' – into a familiarly modern one of masculine domination.[20] Most recently, Richard Marggraf-Turley's *Keats's Boyish Imagination* daringly explores 'immaturity' as the emphatic site of Keats's political consciousness.[21] The purpose of this volume is to develop and extend these recent enquiries by focusing on his often fraught exploration of masculinity across a range of genres: attempts at epic, narrative poems, the odes and his letters.

II. 'WHAT IS LOVE?': THE REAL AND THE ETHEREAL

> And what is love? It is a doll dressed up
> For idleness to cosset, nurse, and dandle;
> A thing of soft misnomers, so divine
> That silly youth doth think to make itself
> Divine by loving, and so goes on
> Yawning and doting a whole summer long,
> Till Miss's comb is made a pearl tiara,
> And common Wellingtons turn Romeo boots.
> Then Cleopatra lives at Number Seven,
> And Antony resides in Brunswick Square.
> Fools! if some passions high have warmed the world,
> If queens and soldiers have played deep for hearts,
> It is no reason why such agonies
> Should be more common than the growth of weeds.
> Fools! make me whole again that weighty pearl
> The queen of Egypt melted, and I'll say
> That ye may love in spite of beaver hats.

This brief poem was given the title 'Modern Love' by Keats's editors when it first came to prominence in the mid-nineteenth century. It provides a rare glimpse of Keats using the contemporary scene of fashionable love for creative effect. For the most part, he leaves such a scene behind in preference for an idealised realm of romance, often located within a pagan, classical mythology or a chivalric medievalism. 'Wellingtons' and 'beaver hats' – the modish accoutrements of Regency ladies of fashion – are not the usual stuff of his poetry. For all of this poem's pert mockery of fashionable young lovers and its apparent display of a more tough-minded attitude, however, it manifests one of the most important tendencies in Keats's poetry: the belief in love as a transformative power capable of translating the lover into something approaching the divine. Despite scoffing at the figure of the 'silly youth', the poem explores, in typical Keatsian fashion, the nature of love's metamorphosis. By the end of the poem, it's almost as if the supposedly cynical speaker has fallen in with the idealism of love even as he asks for Cleopatra's pearl to be reconstituted.

If this is Keats playing John Donne, it shares in Donne's assumption of love's alchemy, but is less convincing in its articulation of a scornful cynicism. What the poem also reveals in its repetition of the word 'common' is Keats's deep-seated agitation at the prevailing scene of manners, conventions and values which surrounded him as a lover and as a poet. For a poet who often inclines instinctively towards the democratic, there's a worrying degree of contempt for the common here which betrays the precariousness of the poem's attack on idle young lovers. Their seemingly desperate (and potentially ridiculous) attempts to find romance in their rootedly contemporary lives are born of an idealism of which the speaker seems only too keenly aware. For the assumption which lurks beneath this half-humorous attack on his contemporary lovers is that love needs defining and redefining; it needs to be removed from this reductive, belittling context if it is to be understood for the powerful and sacred thing Keats believes it to be. Instead of being thought of as a frivolous and infantile dressing up, love should be seen as an essential aspect of the soul. The question 'What is love?', as conceived here, soon turns, then, into a question of how best to represent love in poetry so as to redeem it from its contemporaneity.

Keats's rich exploration of romance is thus, as we shall see, a way of negotiating between the contemporary and the wider historical domain of poetry. 'Modern Love', as it was anachronistically titled, provides an all too brief insight within the body of Keats's poetry of his unease with contemporary society, particularly with its fashionability. In the *Letters*, on the other hand, such unease repeatedly finds articulate expression. This is all the more important to an understanding of Keats's achievement as a love poet because he insistently associates women with this uncongenial modishness of Regency culture. This conflation of woman with the predominant fashionable spirit of the times is recurrent in his correspondence. As Keats's literary ambition and sense of vocation take hold it is possible to trace an increasing sense of irritation and deliberate distancing of himself from a world of youthful fashion and entertainments. Having once had something of a penchant for dressing up and sporting a naval costume as well as growing fashionable whiskers,[22] Keats increasingly distances himself from the prevailing fashion-conscious manners and display of his society. He seems particularly aggressively disposed towards dandies – rather like his friend Hazlitt, whose own more self-professedly 'manly' form of lower-middle-class masculinity leads him to castigate them as a sign of the feminisation of English culture. According to Hazlitt, they are a blight upon the national character and he suggests, in keeping with his more robust form of masculinity's affinity with pugilism and other manly sports, that they must be 'trample[d] into the earth like grasshoppers'.[23] Keats seems to be engaging in self-mockery when telling his brother George in relation to his invitation to a birthday dance that 'I shall be the only dandy there.' His explanation – 'I merely comply with the invitation that the party may no[t] be entirely destitute of a specimen of that Race'[24] – indicates something of his real antipathy. An entry in his friend Charles Brown's 'Walks in the North' (the journey on which he famously accompanied Keats through the Lake District and into Scotland in the summer of 1818) provides further evidence of the degree to which the young men of Keats's friendship group dissociated themselves from what they saw as a less manly form of masculinity:

> When wound up to enthusiasm for natural objects, it is like enduring a direct act of hostility to meet with something brought from the depths of sophistication. At the inn here near mid-day, came a yawning dandy from his bed-room, and sat at his breakfast reading a bouncing novel! (*Letters*, I, 431)

Keats's relationship with his fiancée Fanny Brawne seems from the outset to have been problematically enmeshed in this problem of stylishness and fashion. When introducing her in a letter to his brother George and his wife Georgiana, the description of her appearance is soon followed by a confession of critique: 'I was forced lately to make use of the term *Minx* – this is I think no[t] from any innate vice but from a penchant she has for acting stylishly. I am however tired of such style and shall decline any more of it [...]' (*Letters*, II, 13). Much later in the relationship, Keats even agonises over the degree to which their group of friends will submit them to gossipy attention: 'Good gods what a shame it is our Loves should be so put into the microscope of a Coterie' (*Letters*, II, 293). The terms of their relationship are profoundly defined in opposition to this acute sense of being talked about and subject to the gaze of opinion. At this same time, Keats was developing a strong countervailing historical sense of seeing beyond the limits of his contemporary social scene:

> We with our bodily eyes see but the fashion and Manners of one country for one age – and then we die – Now to me manners and customs long since passed whether among the Babylonians or the Bactrians are as real, or eveven more real than those among which I now live – My thoughts have turned lately this way [...]   (*Letters*, II, 18)

It is not surprising, then, that he should write to Fanny herself earnestly intent on redefining the terms under which their relationship must proceed: 'If we love we must not live as other men and women do – I cannot brook the wolfsbane of fashion and foppery and tattle' (*Letters*, II, 291). The letters to Fanny Brawne – like many of Keats's poems – are daring explorations of a new mode of romance. But the danger of this position is also clearly apparent in Keats's conjuring the reality of the customs of the Bactrians and the Babylonians. Isolating oneself from one's contemporary culture is a real possibility here. The risk of his losing himself in the arcane and the historically obscure is always offset, however, by the attraction of seeing through 'our bodily eyes'.

The link Keats often makes between fashionable modes of masculinity and femininity and the nature of woman is revealing of one of his major achievements as a poet: his setting up a realm of romance in opposition to dominant contemporary mores. Only by analysing Keats's often angry, intemperate, and sometimes contradictory, rejections of his immediate cultural context, can one begin to understand why his poetry takes the form it does. But to suggest that Keats is solely concerned with an idealising representation of love through the use of abstracted romance and classical mythology would also misrepresent his case. The tension evident between ordinary contemporary experience and the higher possibilities of passion in 'What is love? It is a doll dressed up' remains a constant feature of Keats's output. So does humour and teasing playfulness. Throughout his brief career he produced poems of a bawdy and humorous kind which deploy accessible, popular and folksy verse forms. Poems such as 'Give me Women, Wine, and Snuff', 'Hither, hither, love', 'O Blush not so! O blush not so!', 'Where be ye going, you Devon maid?' and 'Over the hill and over the dale' among others, form a significant body of work which is produced side by side with poems of more formal, epic ambition. As we shall see, even some of the most notable canonical poems contain, as part of their daring exploration of sexuality, significant elements of bawdy pleasure.

'Where be ye going, you Devon Maid?' and 'Over the hill and over the dale' were both composed when Keats was staying at Teignemouth in Devon during the wet spring of 1818. The poems appear in letters to friends: the first to the painter Benjamin Robert Haydon, the second to James Rice. By way of introduction to Haydon, Keats writes 'Here's some doggrel for you {-} perhaps you would like a bit of B-hrell–' which his friend interpreted as 'Bitchrell'. And, after his transcription of the poem, he suggests that 'it will be safe with you if worthy to put among my Lyrics' (*Letters*, I, 251). The context for 'Over the hill and over the dale' is more difficult to fathom. In the letter, Keats writes of his encounter with 'little Barmaids' and their previous acquaintance with his correspondent. Both poems, then, are deeply embedded in a process of male bonding and, especially the latter, an expectation of sexual encounter. In the poems themselves, the encounter is between the speaker of the poem and the young girls from the lower ranks of society. Taken in isolation, the poems lack the evidence of this other audience: the relaying of a scene of sexual encounter to a male friend. One might add here that the poems might also be said to stand in for the kind of actual accounts of sexual liaisons which we might expect in a correspondence between young men. To this extent, the two quatrain poems which Keats offers to his friends are highly mediated, stylised and indirect versions of sexual conquests. They demonstrate Keats's ability to engage in a kind of folk-song bawdy which depends upon a sexual knowingness and innuendo.

The second poem begins in a fairly innocent manner, with a jaunty pastoral quaintness to it:

> Over the hill and over the dale,
> And over the bourn to Dawlish –
> Where gingerbread wives have a scanty sale
> And gingerbread nuts are smallish
>
> (ll. 1–4)

But this soon turns to the explicitly bawdy with the introduction of 'Rantipole Betty' – where 'rantipole' means 'rakish' – 'kick[ing] up her petticoats fairly' and the speaker's suggestion that 'I'll be Jack if you will be Jill'. The rest of the poem suggests an alfresco sexual liaison repeatedly urged on by the male speaker, while the young girl is described as a 'venus' or prostitute. The poem ends with a sense of longing – 'O who wouldn't hie to Dawlish fair' – and the suspicion that 'rumpl[ing] the daisies there' stands as a slang euphemism for this kind of sex. Similarly, in the poem sent to Haydon, the speaker's pressing the 'tight little fairy – just fresh from the dairy' whose 'junkets' he loves 'hugely' to 'give [him] some cream if I ask it' – also suggests the possibility of a bawdy sexual slang underlying the poem's rather arch pastoral innocence. Both lyrics exhibit an isolated male speaker pressing a lower-class young girl for sexual favours expressed in the quasi-pastoral terms of country produce. Read in the context of their first appearance in letters to close friends, the poems demonstrate more of the power of shared homosociality than the private anguish of a romantic longing.

Such examples of creative playfulness also indicate the extent to which Keats was not working in isolation, but, first of all, within a small coterie of friends and acquaintances; and, more generally, in what is increasingly recognised as a distinctive group of writers with a significant number of shared aesthetic values – the so-called 'Cockney School'. As Jeffrey Cox has persuasively argued, the importance of this group for Keats has long been undervalued in an attempt to clear his poetry from the savage attacks of damning reviewers in *Blackwood's Edinburgh Magazine* and the *Quarterly*. Reviewers in these conservative journals consistently used the derogatory label 'Cockney' to undermine what they regarded as the threat of liberal writers engaged in an aesthetic of pagan classicism and the erotic which conflicted with their championing of an orthodoxly Christian moral landscape poetics based on the

pastoral poetry of Wordsworth. It is now possible, however, following Jeffrey Cox's lead, to see Keats's poetic output within its
appropriate setting alongside the related writings of Leigh Hunt,
John Hamilton Reynolds, Barry Cornwall, Horace Smith and
Cornelius Webb.[25]

Despite his concerted efforts to create a realm of romance
removed from the realism of his contemporary world, many of
Keats's poems are occasional in nature and are dedicated to members of his close circle of family and friends. He engaged in sonnet-
writing competitions with Leigh Hunt, and 'On the Grasshopper
and Cricket' was famously produced in under fifteen minutes in
one such challenge in December 1816. 'On Receiving a Laurel
Crown', 'On Seeing a Lock of Milton's Hair' and 'To the Nile' were
produced in similar circumstances. Of the poems dedicated to
members of his coterie, 'To J. H. Reynolds, Esq.' is a verse epistle
in couplets – originally sent as part of a letter – which explicitly
negotiates between the realm of romance and the more everyday
world of a relationship between friends. The poem records the
'shapes and shadows' which come before the eyes of the poet as he
lies in bed. To that extent it is entirely characteristic of Keats's
interest in 'waking dreams', the seeing of visions and fancies in a
state of mind which lies at the edge of consciousness. In this
instance, the visions are threatening, negative and ostensibly uncreative, and Keats dismisses them as he demonstrates his typical
attraction towards gestures of self-extinction in his sentiment to his
friend that: 'You know I'd sooner be a clapping bell / To some
Kamchatkan missionary church, / Than with these horrid moods be
left in lurch.'[26] Wishing his friend a recovery from his illness, Keats
looks to cure himself of this negative melancholy by finding
'refuge' in 'new romance'. The poem offers an intimate, revealing
and, at the same time, relaxed account of his state of mind to a
friend in an area which hovers uneasily between creativity and
what today we might refer to as mental health. Friendship between
the two men is sufficiently confident and intimate to include the
capricious and disturbing nature of the mind as it attempts to
restore itself with the act of male bonding in the communication of
the letter and in its determination to seek out the refuge of
romance.

'To J[ames] R[ice]', a Shakespearean sonnet dedicated to another
close friend, illustrates the depth of feeling in such male friendship.
The opening quatrain deals in the thrill of reunion in a way which

might be thought of as more likely in a romantic attachment:

> O that a week could be an age, and we
>   Felt parting and warm meeting every week,
> Then one poor year a thousand years would be,
>   The flush of welcome ever on the cheek ...
>   (ll. 1–4)

Here the attention to the circulation of the blood in blushing (often associated with Keats's love poetry) serves equally well to capture the intensity of male-bonded friendship. As the sonnet builds to its climactic couplet, it pauses in the twelfth line to consider the possibility of the 'souls' of the two friends existing in 'one eternal pant!' The origins of the sonnet form in Petrarchan love poetry have here been turned to account in a poem which seems confident about maintaining a distinction between the homosocial and the homoerotic, but which has appropriated the language of passion to register the strength of feeling between friends. And even here, as in the epistle to John Hamilton Reynolds, Keats plays off the contingencies and logistics of maintaining a friendship – all its complex meetings and partings – against his sense of the metaphysical or eternal. As in that poem's exotic conjuring of the remote peninsula of Kamchatka, Keats once more gestures excitedly towards the 'Ind!' and the 'rich Levant!'

The degree to which Keats's poetry is steeped in the business of wooing and romance can be measured by the two sonnets 'On Fame' which he wrote at the peak of his powers in late April 1819, immediately prior to the famous odes. In these poems, he uses the discourse of a male lover in order to explore his poetic ambitions. In the first of these, fame is described as 'a wayward girl' who 'will still be coy / To those who woo her with too slavish knees, / But makes surrender to some thoughtless boy.'[27] This is the language used between men to discuss their conduct with women where love is always a potential weakness, at best a condition that can be alleviated through the advice of one's more experienced fellows. Keats's poem ends with the fiction of just such an outsider's view: 'Ye artists lovelorn! Madmen that ye are, / Make your best bow to her and bid adieu – / Then, if she likes it, she will follow you.'[28] In the second sonnet, which carries the proverbial 'You cannot eat your cake and have it too' as its epigraph, Keats develops the idea of passion's wasting energy in order to make his comparison with fame. But here he ventures into more unconventional territory by feminising the figure of the poet. The 'fevered' man who is at the mercy of this passion is, by line 4, compared to a woman whose 'fair name' is 'rob[bed]' of its 'maidenhood'. The poem proceeds with a series of feminine possibilities, including a rose, a naiad and a 'meddling elf', before returning by way of confirmation to the subject of 'man' in its conclusion. For Keats, not only love itself and poetry, but also fame can be construed in the terms of romance conducted through the masculine perspective of homosocial advice: fame, as much as poetry, takes on the dynamics and the language of heterosexual romance.

Friendship, then, plays a major part in Keats's processes of poetic production. It not only provides the subject of many poems, but it motivates and provides the spur to their composition and structures many of the representations of self and passion which take place within them. By also analysing Keats's complex responses to women and fashion within this male-dominated coterie – the way in which this influences his attitude to audience, fame and the nature of poetry itself – we will arrive at a more nuanced appreciation of his relationship to issues of gender. Certainly, without this awareness it is all too easy to oversimplify Keats's attachment to and immersion in certain feminine and feminised aspects of the literary culture which surrounded him.

III. KEATS AND WOMEN

On the evidence of his letters, Keats's attitude to women seems to share the doubleness of perspective which we have already identified in his love poetry. He sees them from the position of a 'man of the world' – with all that the phrase implies – as well as from the position of an 'Eternal being'. At its best, his poetry creatively inhabits this duality in its relish of the spiritual sublimation of passion and its excitement at the prospect of sexual pleasure. In a number of poems, as we shall see, Keats even pushes the juxtaposition of these two to the extreme by making the corporeal side of things decidedly grotesque. This is the case with 'The Eve of St Agnes' where he frames his youthful lovers Madeline and Porphyro with a disturbing reminder of their aching mortality in the decaying figures of the suffering beadsman and the aged Angela. Lamia, of course, represents his most daring representation of his conflicted configuration of woman. In his sympathetic portrayal of this serpent/woman

Keats includes in one uncanny form many of the diverse figures of woman who feature in his writing. Lamia combines the mythical nymph with the courtesan, the victim of violent male sexual passion with the emasculating power of a Circe. In his letters, Keats articulates the related anxieties, fears, and frustrations as well as the aggressive tendencies towards women that one might expect from a young man lacking sexual confidence and decidedly more used to the company of men in the form of his brothers and his friends. In a letter to Keats's publisher John Taylor, his friend John Hamilton Reynolds reveals the extent to which derogatory comments on women were a fashionable expectation in correspondence between men. 'The weather here is as changeable as a Woman,' he writes, adding in a parenthesis which suggests some unease with the fashion, that: '(this is the established style of manly comparison – and therefore I adopt it.)'[29] Keats's commentaries are situated within such a conventional discourse between men, but go beyond it. The problem of woman for Keats is also compounded by the threat women represent to the successful fulfilment of his vocation as a poet. His ambition in the field of poetic romance is starkly at odds with his fraught desire for romance in real life. This is all too agonisingly and movingly apparent at various points in his relationship with Fanny Brawne where financial constraints only add to the problem.

One of Keats's most revealing and most disturbing commentaries on his attitude towards women occurs in a letter to his friend Benjamin Bailey dated 18 and 22 July 1818. There's a surprising degree of candour here and it is coupled with an unusual degree of self-diagnosis. As one might expect from Keats, there's also an extremely intense sense of the individuated self surrounded by others in the uncomfortable and embarrassing context of the domestic interior of polite society:

> I am certain I have not a right feeling towards Women – at this moment I am striving to be just to them but I cannot – Is it because they fall so far beneath my Boyish Imagination? When I was a Schoolboy I though[t] a fair Woman a pure Goddess, my mind was a soft nest in which some one of them slept though she knew it not – I have no right to expect more than their reality. I thought them ethereal above Men – I find then perhaps equal – great by comparison is very small – Insult may be inflicted in more ways than by Word or action – one who is tender of being insulted does not like to think of an insult against another – I do not like to think insults in a Lady's

Company – I commit a Crime with her which absence would not have not known – Is it not extraordinary? When among Men I have no evil thoughts, no malice, no spleen – I feel free to speak or to be silent – I can listen and from every one I can learn – my hands are in my pockets I am free from all suspicion and comfortable. When I am among Women I have evil thoughts, malice spleen – I cannot speak or be silent – I am full of Suspicions and therefore listen to no thing – I am in a hurry to be gone – You must be charitable and put all this perversity to my being disappointed since Boyhood – yet with such feelings I am happier alone among Crowds of men, by myself or with a friend or two – With all this trust me Bailey I have not the least idea that Men of different feelings and inclinations are more short sighted than myself [...]   (*Letters*, I, 341)

Some of the key terms and structures of Keats's representation of women and gender relations are already clearly evident in this remarkably honest confession to a friend. The split Keats identifies and attempts to explain by reference to his 'Boyish imagination' – between woman as idealised, imaginary and ethereal, and woman as she is in the reality of polite social interaction – underscores much of his best poetry. So, too, does his unsuccessful struggle to grant women equal status. Instead, as in traditional and still familiar forms of chivalry, they are either more or less than their male counterparts – never the same. Women here are, even more disappointingly, the measure of humanity's incapacity for transformation, refinement or idealisation. Interestingly, Keats locates the origin of this disappointment in boyhood, at once signalling the process of becoming a man and recognising his own particular problem within that standard process of maturation. What the passage also most spectacularly reveals is the degree to which Keats is disturbed by the figure of woman: a figure, as he articulates it, which inhabits the fault-line of his idealism. As a result, he details what can only be described as a profoundly unproductive form of embarrassment for a poet often celebrated for his creative exploration of that condition. Taking him at his own word, Keats's responsiveness to woman here manifests itself in the production of negative thoughts which he goes as far as defining as 'crime', 'evil' and 'malice'. Perhaps the most surprising thing – as well as the most healthy – is his recognition that this is 'perversity'. Typically, his response is to retreat into the company of men – either indiscriminately in 'crowds' or by himself 'with a friend or two'. Isolation among the generality of men or homosocial bonding are equally preferable to the company of woman to the anxious Keats. The passage ends with a peace-offering to men like Bailey who wish to enter into marriage: Keats does not think less of them for wishing to do so. Explaining the peculiar nature of his social sensitivity and the disabling consequences of his disappointed idealism, Keats sets himself apart from the conventional mainstream of lower-middle-class masculinity.

Only a month earlier, Keats had written to Bailey explaining how his extremely close relationship with his brothers had determined his attitude to women: 'My Love for my Brothers from the early loss of our parents and even for earlier Misfortunes has grown into a affection "passing the Love of Women" – I have been ill temper'd with them, I have vex'd them – but the thought of them has always stifled the impression that any woman might otherwise have made upon me' (*Letters*, I, 293). Quoting a biblical phrase (from the book of Samuel), Keats once again signals the exceptional nature of his masculinity, his commitment to a form of male bonding which still allows him the prospect of writing poems and even indulging in the fantasy of 'the glory of dying for a great human purpose'. His confinement to male society is not thought of as a limit, but is immediately equated with the ambition and possible fulfilment of heroic enterprise. Even here, however, Keats is forced into recognising the presence of his brother George's wife, Georgiana. Typically, she turns out to be an exceptional form of femininity. Though: 'Women must want Imagination and they may thank God for it,' Georgiana, perhaps unsurprisingly, turns out to be 'the most disinterrested [*sic*] woman I ever knew'. Her happiness, he adds, is 'the most pleasant and the most extraordinary thing in the world' (*Letters*, I, 293). Woman, in the person of Georgiana, is, then, struck between a lesser category defined in traditional metaphysical terms and exceptionality.

Something of the same anxious withdrawal from contact with women and from the standard social expectations of marriage is evident in a brief passage from a letter to his brother George in October 1818. It begins with a typical Keatsian expression of the poet's extraordinary self-professed capacity for self-isolation and self-absorption:

> I melt into the air with a voluptuousness so delicate that I am content to be alone – Things combined with the opinion I have of the generallity of women – who appear to me as children to whom I

would rather give a Sugar Plum than my time, form a barrier against Matrimony which I rejoice in. [...] You see therre is nothing spleenical in all this. The only thing that can ever effect me personally for more than one short passing day, is any doubt about my powers for poetry ... (*Letters*, I, 404)

Keats's description of himself here as 'melt[ing] into the air with voluptuousness' appropriates the language of sexual union in order to justify and, in one sense, prove his ability to function as an undistracted, ambitious poet dedicated to his literary vocation. To describe one's being alone as a form of 'voluptuousness' is a radical reinscription of categories. In support of this, 'melt', as used in 'The Eve of St Agnes', is Keats's preferred word for the act of sexual consummation.

Even if, as his biographers have argued, Keats managed to alleviate his difficulty with women by increasing his contact with them, his profound sense of loss and disappointment focused on the figure of woman was apt to surface throughout the remainder of his short life. During 1819, he was assiduously reading and annotating Burton's *The Anatomy of Melancholy* – one of the main sources for his narrative poem 'Lamia'. Against a passage where Burton asserts that, 'Love, universally taken, is defined to be desire', he wrote the following words:

> Here is the old plague spot: the pestilence, the raw scrofula. I mean that there is nothing disgraces me in my own eyes so much as being one of a race of eyes, nose and mouth beings in a planet called the earth who all from Plato to Wesley have always mingled goatish, winnyish, lustful love with the abstract adoration of the deity.[30]

Once more, there is a metaphysically defined disappointment: the promise of the perfectability of the soul taken away by the animalistic tendencies of the body. The combination of soul and body is polarised as a disturbing opposition between 'lustful love' and 'abstract adoration'. Keats articulates a profound sense of personal abjection – 'disgraces me in my own eyes' – with a universalising sense of shame which takes us beyond misogyny into a realm of Swiftian misanthropy. In a letter to his friend the artist Benjamin Robert Haydon, he comes even closer to a Swiftian position in his confession that: 'I admire Human Nature but I do not like *Men* – I should like to compose things honourable to Man – but not fingerable over by *Men*' (*Letters*, I, 415). This represents a significantly modified view from that engendered by Burton's text, but the telling use of the word 'fingerable' registers the intensity of his shame of the body, even when, as in this context, he is writing about his anxiety at presenting his writing to the public. It seems, then, that Keats may be reacting strongly against the premise of Burton's definition of love as desire; or against what he takes to be the negative truth of the statement – that love for him, unfortunately, turns out to be desire. Either way, the conflation of love and desire would have serious repercussions for a poet writing within a coterie defined by its daring celebration of the erotic and whose own poetic output has been rightly celebrated for his championing of sexual passion as a form of spiritual progression and fulfilment.

In an altogether more frivolous and light-hearted exchange with his brother in a letter of 18 September 1819, Keats assiduously and accurately transcribed a lengthy passage of Burton's text which largely consisted of the itemising of the parts of woman's body perceived misogynistically as subject to corruption and decay. Keats offers this to his brother George in the hope that he might be 'very much amused'. It is, he adds, a 'feu de joie', or 'fire of joy', by which he presumably means to indicate an enjoyable piece of satire. The passage is prefaced with the proposition that 'Every Lover admires his Mistress though she be very deformed of herself.' There follows a considerable list of deformities, including:

> pendulis mammis her dugs like two double jugs, or else no dugs in the other extream, bloody-falln fingers, she have filthy, long, unpaired, nails, scabbed hands or wrists, a tan'd skin, a rotten carcass, crooked back, she stoops, is lame, splea footed, as slender in the middle as a cow in the wast, gowty legs, her ankles hang over her shooes, her feet stink, she breed lice, a meer changeling, a very monster, an aufe imperfect, her whole complexion savors, an harsh voice, incondite gesture, vile gate, a vast virago, or an ugly tit, a slug, a fat fustilugs, a trusse, a long lean rawbone, a Skeleton, a Sneaker ...
>
> (*Letters*, II, 191)

The young poet who prided himself on an acute sense of the grotesque obviously thrills to this lexicon of abuse and eventually signs off to his brother with: 'There's a dose for you – fine!', itself a measure of the pronounced homosocial bonding between the two men, given its context in a letter also addressed to his brother's wife. Such an extensive rhetoric for the monstrous variety of woman's corrupt body must have been formative in his thinking about the central figure of his narrative involving the man-devouring serpent-woman Lamia. Even in the ostensibly relaxed context of this male-bonded humour, Keats is seemingly attracted to this portrayal of love's blindness, its capacity for a negatively defined translation of the self.

Such commentaries from the *Letters* represent the most disturbing and negative of Keats's attitudes towards women, although, as I have suggested, they reveal a certain specific structuring of the figure of woman in relation to ideas of love and the spiritual nature of its transformations. According to the structure of his disappointed idealism, the figure of woman represents the point of greatest disturbance: the tempting hindrance to heroic enterprise and spiritual fulfilment. That Keats wishes to operate on this higher, metaphysical level and not just on the social-sexual level certainly complicates the issue. The split governing the figure of woman in his writing is determined by this distinction between the ideal and the real, or, as he might put it, between the 'ethereal' and the real.

In terms of coping with real women under what he clearly saw as the restrictive socio-sexual conventions of his society and social class, Keats could also resort to something of a Platonic defensiveness. Even when inevitably forced into some kind of relatively intimate or sustained social contact with individual women, Keats seems determined to give them exceptional status and to remove them from what he sees as the distracting, compromising and threatening issue of sexual desire. He writes to his brother George about his fraught liaisons with Isabella Jones as follows: 'I have no libidinous thought about her – she and your George are the only women à peu près de mon age whom I would be content to know for their mind and friendship alone' (*Letters*, I, 403). While this statement seems to be offered in order to reassure his brother that he is not entangled in a sexual relationship with this particular woman, it betrays, to an extraordinary degree, the overwhelming presence of sex in his admission that all other women of his age *do* engender libidinous thoughts in him. Keeping his idea of woman, even in this self-confessedly exceptional case, confined to an abstracted, idealised, or safely aestheticised realm proves to be rather difficult.

One of the most interesting examples of this struggle is provided by Keats's response to an acquaintance of the 'Miss Reynoldses'. These sisters represent a form of femininity which fills Keats with severe irritation. When their cousin Jane Cox comes to visit, Keats is alert to the animosity she engenders in her more proper, if frivolous, cousins. The young woman also clearly makes an intense impression upon the young poet. In writing about her to his brother George, however, Keats is very careful to define the nature of the impact she has made upon him. Even allowing for the possibility that Keats is guarding himself against the suggestion of succumbing to her charms and playing strategically with his brother, there's a powerful definition of another role for woman within his thinking here. He obviously sees her as representative of a certain kind of worldly, but aestheticised femininity:

> When she comes into a room she makes an impression the same as the Beauty of a Leopardess. She is too fine and too concious of her Self to repulse any Man who may address her – from habit she thinks that nothing *particular*. I always find myself more at ease with such a woman; the picture before me always gives me a life and animation which I cannot possibly feel with any thing inferiour – I am at such times too much occupied in admiring to be awkward or on a tremble. I forget myself entirely because I live in her. You will by this time think I am in love with her; so before I go any further I will tell you I am not – she kept me awake one Night as a tune of Mozart's might do – I speak of the thing as a passtime and an amuzement than which I can feel none deeper than a conversation with an imperial woman the very 'yes' and 'no' of whose Lips is to me a Banquet. [...] I like her and her like because one has no *sensations* – what we both are is taken for granted [...] They call her a flirt to me – What a want of knowledge? she walks across a room in such a manner that a Man is drawn towards her with a magnetic Power. This they call flirting! they do not know things. they do not know what a Woman is.   (*Letters*, I, 395)

Leaving aside the predatory possibilities of this description, Keats self-evidently prefers the breach of social decorum and propriety which such a self-parading form of femininity effects. Instead of the embarrassing unease and uncertainty created by conventional forms of modesty, Jane Cox's egotism – at least according to Keats – releases him from the burden of etiquette and allows him to engage in an apparently de-sexualised form of aesthetic appreciation. This is soon reduced to a lower level kind of artistic admiration. Though Mozart is invoked, being kept awake by a tune is not an impression of the highest order. In case there should be any doubt, the impression she has made is soon relegated to a mere 'amuzement' or 'passtime'. The phrase 'I like her and her like' cleverly reduces the first possibility of 'like' by punning proximity to its dismissive second. The last three sentences of the extract are perhaps the most intriguing and challenging. Keats, for all his recently professed awkwardness and disabling self-consciousness in the presence of women, now dares to define 'what a woman is' against the judgement of other young women. Such a dangerously confident pronouncement seems to stem from the distinction he makes a few sentences later between 'the worldy, theatrical and pantominical' and 'the unearthly, spiritual and etherial'. 'What a woman is' according to Keats in this context – as the phrase indicates – clearly relates to the first category of the 'worldy'. He even turns the category to punning, sexual account as he jokes reassuringly to his brother: 'As a Man in the world I love the rich talk of a Charmian; as an eternal Being I love the thought of you. I should like her to ruin me and I should like you to save me' (*Letters*, I, 396). The joke also, of course, risks collapsing the pretension that this is a non-sexual admiration.

Keats's writing of this encounter with a young woman also provides an interesting example of the exploration of the self in relation to the presence and the absence of ego: the latter often being thought of, as we have already seen, as synonymous with and characteristic of his kind of poetic creativity. Frequently, it is spoken of as if it operated in a vacuum – Keats's talent for self-abnegation or loss of ego being an ability which can be exercised at will and in isolation. From the evidence of his letters, however, we can see, as in this instance, that such states of consciousness operate in tandem with other egos and in specific social contexts – often in a room with people. Here, the reciprocity of this phenomenon has an added significance because of the intensely gendered nature of the encounter. Keats relieves himself of the anxiety induced by his self-consciousness in the face of young ladies due to the overwhelming presence of a young woman who breaches decorum by her abiding egotism and self-display. He is allowed to 'forget himself', as he puts it, precisely because of the dominance of this female ego. He is saved from embarrassment because Jane Cox is so obviously a beautiful and, at the same time, sexual being. The certainty of sexuality liberates Keats from the ambivalence of social decorum and then enables him, if we take him at his word, to contain that sexual response by aestheticising it. As we have just seen, however, the claim to have removed oneself from 'sensations' doesn't exclude the possibility of being sexually 'ruined' by such a woman.

Such playful doubling is entirely characteristic of Keats's letter-writing which I discuss in the final chapter of this study. As if anticipating the danger of readers oversimplifying such statements, Keats writes about women failing to understand the behaviour of his friend Benjamin Bailey: 'this may teach them [women] that the man who redicules romance is the most romantic of Men – that he who abuses women and slights them – loves them the most' (*Letters*, II, 67). The insight into his friend reveals much about himself.

If Keats's accounts of his self-diagnosed problems with women and of his actual encounters with them provide us with an invaluable insight into the way in which he negotiates between aesthetics and sexuality, the letters also offer ample evidence of the way in which the discourses of gender and aesthetics overlap and react upon each other creatively. As we have just seen, Keats can compare a woman of his acquaintance to an 'amuzement' equivalent to a bothering 'tune of Mozart's' in close proximity to a provocatively confident declaration of 'what a woman is'. At other points in his correspondence, in relation to his reading of Shakespeare and Milton's *Paradise Lost* in preparation for writing *Hyperion* and 'Lamia', he confesses that he 'look[s] upon fine Phrases like a Lover', (*Letters*, II, 139) once again suggesting that literary ambition is a chosen replacement for romance. Given the assumption that romance and literary ambition contend for the same male energy, it is not surprising that the discourse of one is so readily found in the context of the other. At one point, Keats conceives of poetry not simply as his Muse, but as if 'she' were his mistress: ' – I know not why Poetry and I have been so distant lately I must make some advances soon or she will cut me entirely' (*Letters*, II, 74). In the other direction, he scornfully observes that: 'I have met <wht> with women whom I really think would like to be married to a Poem and to be given away by a Novel' (*Letters*, II, 127). This negatively perceived feminisation of literary fame also leads him, in a letter to his publisher John Taylor, to equate the public with a disturbing image of a female lover: 'I equally dislike the favour of the public with the love of a woman – they are both a cloying treacle to the wings of independence' (*Letters*, II, 144).

One of the most important tensions within Keats's poetry is apparent in these deeply ambivalent responses to women which reveal most starkly his sense of the limitations of the present and his need to transcend it. The trajectory of his poetic ambitions might, as in the letter to Taylor, identify 'woman' as the real danger to its fulfilment, but the territory of his best poems is as interested in a 'cloying' contact with the physical reality of passion as it is with metaphysical flights of imagination. As will become evident in the chapters which follow, Keats's 'feminine' poetry maintains this double impulse: the search for transcendence coupled with a passionate attachment to the corporeal.

2

Epic Abstraction

Keats's long poems – *Endymion*, *Hyperion* and *The Fall of Hyperion* – form a substantial amount of his creative output and serve as a reminder of his considerable ambition as a poet.[1] In these extraordinary poems, he tests himself out against the most prestigious of genres, the epic and the romance, and against the daunting precedents set by Homer, Ovid, Spenser and Milton. Within his own development as a poet capable of handling the long poem, he displays a struggle with the problem of style, moving between the influence of Spenser and that of Milton. For the purposes of this study, these poems provide an opportunity to see how Keats explores the subject of love to some degree removed and abstracted from the immediate context of his own society and the pressing concerns of his own social milieu and its contemporary forms of gender identity. Dealing in classical myth enables Keats to come at his contemporary society from a refreshingly new angle and to explore sexuality liberated from the stifling propriety of middle-class mores.

Central to Keats's concerns in all of these poems is the power of love and its capacity to radically transform the self. As he moves from *Endymion* to *Hyperion* and to *The Fall of Hyperion*, Keats wrestles with genre, gender and language: from the sensuous, 'feminine' romance of *Endymion* through to the stark, masculine austerity of *The Fall of Hyperion* which he eventually sees as a dead-end. Throughout, he engages with the difficulty of representing a new form of heroism. From the potentially dangerous passivity of the shepherd-king Endymion he moves to a dramatic contest between the unflinching heroic masculinity of the old sun-god Hyperion and the new god of the sun, music, and song: Apollo. The latter's enigmatic metamorphosis into a god forms the tantalising end to his epic fragment in which the role of the poet has been subjected to typically rigorous scrutiny. Throughout, Keats's explorations in the abstracted realm of myth and epic are always agonisingly in touch with mortality, with the aching and suffering selves of the merely human.

I. *ENDYMION*

Endymion: a Poetic Romance is Keats's first extended and completed attempt at epic. The young poet saw it as a 'test, a trial of [his] Powers of Imagination and chiefly of [his] invention'. The task as he envisaged it, was how to 'make 4000 Lines out of one bare circumstance and fill them with Poetry' (*Letters*, I, 169–70). His dogged determination to complete the project of a long poem was matched by his sense of its inevitable immaturity. But in terms of the making of a poet and the sense of capacity to match his ambition the project obviously gave him the confidence and the conviction that he possessed the potential to work on this grand Miltonic scale. In his understandably anxious attempts to write a preface for this ambitious, but flawed epic, Keats modestly comes before his public aware of the poem's shortcomings, but in the hope that his critics will have the good faith to recognise his potential. In the unpublished version of the preface, he gives it the status of an unfinished work: 'So this Poem must rather be considered as an endeavour rather than a thing accomplish'd.'[2] In the version published with the poem in May 1818 Keats is even more apologetic on behalf of his youthful creation. He opens with a seeming apology for bringing *Endymion* to the public gaze before identifying the poem's only too evident display of 'inexperience, immaturity, and every error denoting a feverish attempt, rather than a deed accomplished'.[3] This characterisation of the poem as a 'feverish attempt' chimes with Keats's abiding sense of *Endymion* as the creation of a youthful imagination, a rite of passage which must be gone through so long as it offered sufficient promise of his epic potential.

The published preface to *Endymion* contains a rather precise sense of this youthful promise and its implications for the kind of imperfections to be found in the poem. Here Keats once again ascribes a pathological quality to the poem:

> The imagination of a boy is healthy, and mature imagination of a
> man is healthy; but there is a space of life between, in which the soul

is in a ferment, the character undecided, the way of life uncertain, the ambition thick-sighted: thence proceeds mawkishness, and all the thousand bitters which those men [...] must taste in going over the following pages.[4]

Interestingly, Keats defines the nature of his first writing of epic in terms of a process of maturation: as part of the narrative of becoming a man. The 'feverish attempt' that is *Endymion* represents the blurred transitional state of developing masculinity – 'the space of life between' boy and man. It is characterised by 'fever' and 'ferment' of the soul, a profound agitation which militates against clarity of vision. Ambition itself is here 'thick-sighted', by which Keats presumably also wishes to indicate a lack of specificity of purpose and finesse. In advertising his poem in this way, Keats might seem to be naïvely offering his hostile critics the ammunition with which they can wage their onslaught, but the severe self-criticism also indicates a developing level of self-awareness. It is as if the writing of *Endymion* has been an act of initiation, a rite of passage which leads to the mature poet.

Keats's extremely frank and honest admission of *Endymion*'s immaturity should not diminish our sense of the poem's very particular take on epic and its productive relationship to his later poems. In describing it in its subtitle as a 'poetic romance' Keats might be thought of as aiming below the level of epic, particularly epic of the kind so successfully achieved by Milton in *Paradise Lost*. That the later books especially bear the imprint of his reading of Milton's epic at the time of writing we know from his correspondence. But the project of the poem at its inception might even more particularly be thought of as a reinscription of epic romance. Keats seems to have had in mind a poem which offered an insight into the transformative and redemptive power of love. In that alone it stands in significant relationship to Milton's Christian epic whose argument displays the redeeming power of divine as well as human love. Keats's poem, too, is most emphatically a poem about the nature of the soul, albeit a soul conceived of in unorthodox terms of essences. In this respect, it represents a concerted enquiry into precisely that agitated and uncertain phase of masculinity in which, as he puts it in the preface, 'the soul is in a ferment' and 'the way of life is uncertain'. In both these aspects *Endymion* focuses on a major topic of Keats's concern as a poet.

In addition to its focus on the transformative and redemptive power of romantic love, *Endymion* also conceives of itself as a national epic. This aspect of the poem is often underplayed or even goes largely unnoticed because of the classical and mythical nature of Keats's chosen narrative in which the exotic paganism of the poem has the effect of occluding the poem's concerned Englishness. The ethical power of romantic love is directed throughout the poem at redeeming the poet's native land which is, in turn, defined in specifically pastoral terms. Immediately after announcing in the third paragraph of the poem that the name of Endymion 'has gone / Into my being' Keats aligns his burgeoning creativity with the springtime and the country in which he writes: 'each pleasant scene / Is growing fresh before me as the green / Of our own valleys.'[5] The poem's dedication to the eighteenth-century poet Thomas Chatterton clinches this integral English identity as much as its conjuring of the figure of the youthful poet and the subject of romance. Rather like Wordsworth's epic *The Prelude* which, even in its early verse epistle form, offers itself up in the face of 'times of dereliction and dismay', Keats's poetic romance offers the hopeful prospect of redeeming the time through the timeless beauty of nature. Its famous, almost aphoristic, opening line – 'A thing of beauty is a joy for ever' – is waged against 'despondence, of the inhuman dearth / Of noble natures, of the gloomy days, / Of all the unhealthy and o'er-darkened ways / Made for our searching: yes, in spite of all / Some shape of beauty moves away the pall / From our dark spirits' (*E*, I, ll. 1, 8–13). With this ethical and even socio-political frame in mind, the metamorphic capacity of love, its ability to translate us into other beings and take us to 'heaven's brink', is the deliberate and focused concern of his poem's romantic quest.

The 'bare circumstance' which forms the content of the poem (and which Keats sees himself as elaborating so as to 'fill up' with 4000 lines of poetry) consists of the love between the moon-goddess Diana and the shepherd/king Endymion. The poem's generation of an internalised quest narrative comes about because the hero falls in love with an unknown female form during the course of a dream. Keats multiplies the female figure in the guise of an 'Indian maid' and then Cynthia before Diana reveals to Endymion that all these are really versions of herself. The narrative is thus a test as well as a quest in which the hero ultimately attains immortal status and therefore consummation with his goddess because, ironically, he chooses mortal love over the divine version. He thereby endorses the poem's ethical directive that romantic love leads us to the brink of the divine. Along the way, Endymion struggles with the alienated misery into which the transformative power of love has thrust him. Unhappy consciousness characterises his metamorphosis and generates his quest to find and identify the elusive object of his desire. To this extent, Endymion epitomises the tortured self-consciousness of the poet as much as the tormented lover, and the poem as a whole struggles to measure the enduring power of beauty against the pain and suffering of the world.

In this aspect, *Endymion* articulates the threat to its optimistic belief in the power of romantic love more successfully in its interpolated narrative of Glaucus, Scylla and Circe which forms the bulk of its third book than it does in its main narrative. Here the poem is able to focus more intently on the darker, disturbing and deceptive potential within romantic love. Glaucus's narrative provides a powerful preview of the nightmarish deceptions and wasting of the male body and male identity which later take place in 'La Belle Dame sans Merci' and 'Lamia'. This is the downside to amatory metamorphosis which can only be redeemed through Endymion in conjunction with the happy providence which prevails over his narrative.

Circe successfully tempts Glaucus, though he is in pursuit of Scylla, and the transformation of love is described by him in terms of the promise of ambrosial bliss which results in a strange state of transfixation and disgust. Wanting to 'immerse / [His] fine existence in a golden clime', instead he is taken by Circe 'like a child of suckling time' (*E*, III, ll. 454–6) and suffers an immediate exile from his past. His realisation that it is Circe who has carried out this bewitching transformation of his identity is accompanied by a scene of Spenserian grotesquerie in which she becomes the queen of deformity. This is the 'gross, detestable, filthy mesh' (*E*, III, l. 55) of negatively defined femininity reminiscent of Milton's Sin and Death in *Paradise Lost*, which now defines his existence. He becomes subject or vassal not only to Circe, but, more generally, to the negatively defined characteristics of our human condition: age, pain, loss and suffering. His limbs turn 'Gaunt, withered, sapless, feeble, cramped, and lame' (*E*, III, l. 638). He now becomes the 'aged form' who encounters Endymion. His only release from death is the instruction to 'explore all forms and substances / Straight homeward to their symbol-essences'. Like Endymion's rather vaguely defined pretensions to astronomy (often associated with this classical myth, though here of secondary importance) represented by his falling in love with the moon, Glaucus takes on the burden of the poem's quest to understand the nature of souls and their capacity for transformation and change. He can only be redeemed or 'renovated' by the action of youthful love represented by Endymion directing him back to the light 'where lovely Scylla lies' (*E*, III, l. 720). As well as a restoration to his previous youthful form, this act of reanimation brought about by the power of love constitutes a defeat for death and a victory for the pulses of life.

The 'sovereign power of love' (*E*, II, l. 1) which forms the noble subject of his long poem is not without formidable risk. Keats understands that the potential liberatory force of passion (evident in his call for it to 'unmew / [His] soul') (*E*, I, ll. 132–3) also constitutes a form of dominion over the self and certainly involves the danger of losing oneself in the union with another. Even in his celebration of the creative and renovating power of 'Magic sleep' he is careful to stress the paradox: 'O unconfined / Restraint! Imprisoned liberty!' And, in his justification for taking romantic love as the subject of his epic, Keats foregrounds the daring involved in entering upon such a dangerous form of entanglement. In describing the hierarchy of relationships – or these 'richer entanglements' as he calls them – Keats measures their worth by the degree of threat they represent to the self. These most meaningful of relationships, he argues, are 'far more / Self-destroying' (*E*, I, ll. 453–6, 798–9). Friendship is accorded a significant place in this hierarchy, but it is, ultimately, superseded by romantic love:

> the crown of these
> Is made of love and friendship, and sits high
> Upon the forehead of humanity.
> All its more ponderous and bulky worth
> Is friendship, whence there ever issues forth
> A steady splendour; but at the tip-top,
> There hangs by unseen film, an orbèd drop
> Of light, and that is love: its influence,
> Thrown in our eyes, genders a novel sense,
> At which we start and fret; till in the end,
> Melting into its radiance, we blend,
> Mingle, and so become a part of it –
> Nor with aught else can our souls interknit
> So wingedly.
>
> (*Endymion*, I, ll. 800–13)

For Keats, then, love of this sort constitutes more than an intense confirmation of self: it is rather the loss of the self which he contemplates as it melts, mingles and blends with the larger force. Self-abnegation dominates even the sense of human or sexual relationship in which the lovers are envisaged as 'blending'. The agitated state of 'fret' referred to characterises the excitement, surprise and uncertainty of the self in Keats's state of love. This agitation might easily be equated with precisely that state of feverish ferment of the soul (referred to in the preface) indicative of youth – that stage of development before one has acquired the 'healthy imagination' of the mature man. In the poem itself, this agitated state immediately prior to becoming a man is frequently articulated by one of Keats's favourite words: 'perplexity'. The process of passion is measured by perplexity. By contrast to the image of young love, Lamia has the skill and knowledge to 'unperplex' passion.

It is these elements of daring and danger which provide Keats with the justification for seeing his new form of 'poetic romance' as fulfilling the heroic qualities of classical and traditional epic. In book II of *Endymion* he dares to claim that 'The silver flow / Of Hero's tears, the swoon of Imogen, / Fair Pastorella in the bandit's den, / Are things to brood on with more ardency / Than the death-day of empires'; and he realises the risk to his poetic career in thus 'striving to uprear / Love's standard on the battlements of song' (*E*, II, ll. 30–4, 40–1). Keats provocatively poses the ardour and struggle of romance against the puissance of military epic. He clearly indicates that his territory is the embattled self and its possible dissolution rather than the destruction of armies and empires. There's also a strong historical self-consciousness here which sees the contemporary society in need of renovation and redemption, but lacking the epic power to bring it about. Keats's strong sense of the prevailing power of love and its extraordinary capacity to transform the self is accompanied by a condition of literary belatedness: a conviction that the best of literature has already been produced. In the following passage from book II, for example, there's a resigned fatalism in the face of past literary greatness coupled with a yearning for the truth of romance:

> Ay, the count
> Of mighty Poets is made up; the scroll
> Is folded by the Muses; the bright roll
> Is in Apollo's hand: our dazèd eyes
> Have seen new tinge in the western skies:
> The world has done its duty. Yet, oh yet,

> Although the sun of poesy is set,
> These lovers did embrace, and we must weep
> That there is no old power left to steep
> A quill immortal in their joyous tears
>   (*Endymion,* II, 723–32)

Keats's sense of the metaphysical, quasi-religious power of love is governed by a historical self-consciousness which sees contemporary society characterised by loss in relation to a strategically located deployment of an ancient mythology. Keats looks to Apollo in order to find the appropriate way of addressing and articulating his philosophy of love. In addition to the burden of his love-lorn melancholia, Endymion also has to overcome 'a cold leaden awe' induced by the spectre of history. In book III he encounters 'things / More dead than Morpheus's imaginings'. These include 'Old rusted anchors, helmets, breast-plates large / Of gone sea-warriors' and 'Rudders that for a hundred years had lost / The sway of human hand' – the relics of an anonymous and unrecoverable heroism. He also has to face up to the remnants of an aboriginal, first world which includes, as spectres of pre-Darwinian natural history, 'skeletons of man, / Of beast, behemoth, and leviathan, / And elephant, and eagle, and huge jaw / Of nameless monster' (*E,* III, ll. 121–36).

Keats's poetic romance, then, sets itself up in rivalry with Miltonic heroic epic and at the same time pits itself against what it sees as the age's false standard of ambition and masculine achievement. In book I of the poem Keats writes with the intention of demonstrating how 'love has power to make / Men's being mortal, immortal; to shake / Ambition from their memories ...' (*E,* I, ll. 843–5); while, even more pointedly, the poem engages in explicit social critique at the beginning of book III with its scorn for those 'who lord it o'er their fellow-men / With most prevailing tinsel' (*E,* III, ll. 1–2). The 'enfranchisement' (*E,* III, l. 299) of love is pitched against the prevailing undemocratic spirit of the age.[6]

The reception accorded to Keats's 'poetic romance' by the literary reviews was sufficiently negative to create the myth that Keats was, in some way, killed by his reviewers. Although it is possible to see the poem's subscription to the renovating power of love as lying within a liberal radical ideology of social improvement, antagonistic reviewers preferred, understandably, to opt for a less perceptive, but potentially more destructive mode of personal ridicule. In most of the prominent attacks, Keats is damned by association with his friend and early mentor, the poet and publisher Leigh Hunt. Aggressive Tory reviewers were eager to pick up the scent of someone who had been championed by the so-called king of the Cockneys. Unfortunately, this means that their often easy attacks are focused to an inordinate degree on the poem's 'vulgarity' of diction – the way in which it most obviously declares its affinity with Hunt's own verse, most particularly *The Story of Rimini*.

One of the first attacks, in the *British Critic*, began with the delighted claim that '[t]his is the most delicious poem, of its kind, which has fallen within our notice, and if Mr Leigh Hunt had never written, we believe we might have pronounced it to be *sui generis* without fear of contradiction' before proceeding, on the basis of this association, to refer to its demonstrating 'the gross slang of voluptuousness'.[7] At the same time as he recognises the 'jacobinical' tenor of one of the poem's apostrophes, this reviewer attacks what he sees as its veiled immorality. It is, he warns, a form of 'vicious refinement'.[8] John Gibson Lockhart's attack in the Tory-dominated *Blackwood's Edinburgh Magazine* also has this specifically linguistic focus in its assessment of *Endymion* when it makes the distinction between 'the written language of Englishmen and the spoken jargon of Cockneys'. Lockhart's assault on the poem is a clear attempt to squash Keats's pretensions to work with classical and mythical material. To that end, he deliberately reads *Endymion* very straightforwardly as a portrait of Keats: 'Mr Keats has thoroughly appropriated the character, if not the name. His Endymion is not a Greek shepherd, loved by a Grecian goddess; he is merely a young Cockney rhymester, dreaming a phantastic dream at the full of the moon.'[9]

The often savage John Wilson Croker in the *Quarterly Review* also focuses with fussy intensity on Keats's poetic diction on the basis that the author of *Endymion* is 'a copyist of Mr Hunt' and as such is a 'disciple of the new school of what has been somewhere called Cockney poetry; which may be defined to consist of the most incongruous ideas in the most uncouth language.'[10] In many of these accounts there is a pointed conflation of linguistic and moral concern underscored by class politics. The attack on the 'Cockney' school, as the name itself might suggest, centres on 'vulgarity' which is then used to mobilise the idea of the threat of licentiousness posed by the lower ranks of society exercising their taste in the polite realm of literature. The seeming fastidiousness over poetic diction is thus motivated by the fear of a threat to taste represented in the oxymoronic phrase 'vicious refinement'. The 'uncouth' is here quickly associated with 'voluptuousness'. The sociological aspect of these attacks on Keats's poetic romance finds its most extraordinary and famous manifestation, as we have already seen in chapter 1, in Byron's response to Keats, though his various and dispersed commentaries are removed from the immediate aftermath of the publication of *Endymion*.

In terms of the ambitions and values of Keats's poem, an anonymous reviewer in Leigh Hunt's *Champion* for 8 June 1818, provides what is, in many ways, one of the most perceptive and prescient responses to *Endymion*. (It is likely to have been written by Keats's friend Richard Woodhouse, though it has also been attributed to another friend, John Hamilton Reynolds.) This reviewer recognises the poem's epic ambitions: its handling of mythology, and its dealing in the removed metaphysics of love as a mode of poetry which makes Keats distinctive and difficult in the current Byronic fashion for readers to appreciate. His defensive reaction to what he perceives as the illiberal and unfair response *Endymion* has so far received from the reviews is made with an astute realisation that 'Mr Keats's very excellence [...] will tell against him'.[11] Against the grain of his detractors who immediately castigate the poem for its Cockney affiliations, he sees in Keats's poetic romance a new brand of poetry which removes itself from the personality of the author and the abiding presence of authorial ego in a way which anticipates many of Keats's own developing aesthetic criteria.

The terms of the review are clearly those of an insider: someone taking part in the debate within Keats's close circle of friends and acquaintances. Keats's reaction to what he saw as the egotistical sublime of Milton and Wordsworth and, more generally, to an overly didactic or directed mode of poetic presentation – 'poetry that has a palpable design upon us – and if we do not agree, seems to put its hand into its breeches pocket' (*Letters*, I, 224), as he expresses it in his letters – is interestingly paralleled in the review, though it is given the identity of showmanship rather than that of the preacher or haranguer suggested by Keats's own metaphor. 'The secret of the success of our modern poets', the reviewer claims, 'is their universal presence in their poems – they give every thing the colour of their own feeling'.[12] The reviewer's analysis of Keats's handling of passion in *Endymion* is particularly perceptive in relation to the figure of the poet as an abiding mediating presence. He offers, more generally, an insight into the difficulty contemporary readers may have had in coming to terms with Keats's own distinctive kind of love poetry. And in relation to Keats's ambition in the field of the long poem, this review also focuses on the rather precarious axis of his poetry's combination of sympathy and abstraction, its difficult negotiation of the objective and subjective representation of passion:

> [...] Mr Keats goes out of himself into a world of abstractions: – his passions, feelings, are all as much imaginative as his situations. Neither is it the mere outward signs of passions that are given: there seems ever present some being that was equally conscious of its internal and most secret imaginings. [...] Mr Keats conceives the scene before him, and represents it as it appears. This is the excellence of dramatic poetry; but to feel its truth and power in any other, we must abandon our ordinary feeling and common consciousness, and identify ourselves with the scene. Few people can do this. In representation, which is the ultimate purpose of dramatic poetry, we should feel something of sympathy though we could merely observe the scene, or the gesticulation, and no sound could reach us; but to make an ordinary *reader* sensible of the excellence of a poem, he must be told what the poet felt; and he is affected by him and not by the scene. Our modern poets are the shewmen of their own pictures, and point out its beauties.[13]

This is particularly valuable for its recognition of the importance of abstraction within the workings of Keats's celebrated projective and protean imagination. The label of dramatic poetry is also helpful, if not totally convincing. Most valuable is the realisation that in representing passion in poetry, in all its truthful power, 'we must abandon our ordinary feeling and common consciousness'. There's a shrewd awareness here of the artifice and alienation required in the representation of passion. It demands a new sense of communication and, most particularly, the role of the poet in that act of communication. In order to clinch his sense of Keats's distinctiveness and novelty as a love poet, the reviewer uses as his example from the poem the first meeting between Endymion and Cynthia:

> It is so true to imagination, that passion absorbs every thing. Now, as we have observed, to transfer the mind to the situation of another, to feel as he feels, requires an enthusiasm, and an abstraction, beyond the power or the habit of most people. It is in this way

eloquence differs from poetry, and the same speech on delivery affects people [...] We have certain sympathies with the persona addressing us, and what he feels, we feel in an inferior degree; but he is afterwards to describe to us his passion; to make us feel by *telling us what he felt;* and this is to be done by calculating on the effect on *others'* feelings, and not by abandoning ourselves to our own. If Mr Keats can do this, he has not done it. When he writes of passion, it seems to have possessed him.[14]

Once again, the reviewer is intent on the difficult combination of 'enthusiasm' and 'abstraction'. And, as he extends his argument beyond the confines of poetry, he provides a fascinating glimpse of the communication of passion among men of his circle and social standing. The mediatory nature of the speaker in such situations mirrors the mode which produces 'the secret of the success of our modern poets'. This is the usual and, clearly, the dominant mode. Passion is articulated by the speaker as he relays it to his friends. That italicised phrase *'telling us what he felt'* is most revealing. The language of passion is here already relayed and mediated and works upon a sense of audience. A man articulates his passion not simply as he feels it, but as he imagines its effect upon his audience. Keats, then, is different. He seems to be the passive subject rather the dominating showman; passion possesses him rather than vice versa. But that 'seems' is also shrewd, for it cleverly reserves the possibility of Keats's deliberateness: his artistry and artifice. With this explanation of Keats's innovative mode of representing passion behind him, the reviewer ends by comparing the young poet's mode of creativity with that of Shakespeare by including the suggestion of resemblance between *Endymion* and *Venus and Adonis*. In the flattering comparison with Shakespeare's poem, there's a measured awareness of Keats's poetic talent: a suggestion of great potential rather than, as yet, great achievement.

II. *HYPERION*

For his next epic project, *Hyperion*, Keats developed an idea briefly touched upon in his handling of the mythological materials in *Endymion:* the struggle for supremacy between the ancient Titans and the Olympian gods. Keats's main concern, as his title suggests, is with the sun god Hyperion and his replacement by the new god of the sun, music, and poetry: Apollo. From the fragment of

Hyperion which Keats left uncompleted, it is possible to see his project as an exploration of rival forms of heroism, once more using Milton's precedent in *Paradise Lost* as a model. Whereas Milton there uses Satan in books I and II as a means of challenging and questioning classical, military heroism so that it can be perceived as being supplanted by a new form of Christian heroism embodied not just in Christ, but in Adam, so here Keats's poem addresses a narrative of historical progress which sees Hyperion replaced by Apollo. The 'advance' which this represents is also, as one might expect from Keats, a measure of the nature of their identity – their being, as much as their god-like or heroic status. For all its seeming cosmological import, Keats's epic has this significant psychological basis to its argument.

When he wrote to his friend, the artist Benjamin Robert Haydon, in January 1818, in eager anticipation of the new project of *Hyperion*, Keats was determined to shift the mode of the new poem more firmly into line with classical epic. He sees himself as moving further away from the dangers of mawkishness and sentimentality by opting for what he calls 'a more naked and grecian Manner' (*Letters*, I, 207). There's also a significant shift in terms of the hero's relationship to the narrative in which he's situated. The choice of a god-like hero dictates that the narrative will be a constituent of his being. Although in the earlier poem the divine power of love can be seen as enabling Endymion to transcend his status as a mortal, the narrative can also be said to be largely out of his hands and in those of the goddess Diana. This passivity is reinforced by the perception that Endymion is a lover at the mercy of a narrative of romance rather than a hero of love dictating the progress of his being. And, whereas the shepherd-king Endymion can, in some ways, be read as the passive recipient of providence, here in *Hyperion* knowledge, mind and identity will, Keats suggests to Haydon, be at one with action:

> The march of passion and endeavour will be undeviating – and one great contrast between them will be – that the Hero of [Endymion], – being mortal is led on, like Buonaparte by circumstance; whereas the Apollo in Hyperion being a fore-seeing God will shape his actions like one. (*Letters*, I, 207)

The reference to Buonaparte confirms the extent to which history, including the present, is firmly on the agenda in Keats's narrative of hope and improvement. *Hyperion*, like Milton's epic, takes as its task the explanation of historical change and its relationship to an ethical selfhood. This connection between the experiencing self and the progress of history is a major aspect of Keats's poem. His move towards a more austere, classical, and Miltonic mode serves, then, his attempt to deal with love and the self in a more concertedly abstract way. Whereas the story of *Endymion* provided an opportunity to push the human towards the divine, here we find the human evident within the defeated Titans. This is apparent at the very beginning of *Hyperion* where the gods are in that most Keatsian of psychological states: 'perplexity'.

Keats opens his poem with the old gods already defeated. They exist in a state of forlorn loss with the exception of Hyperion, their one hope of defiance. In their defeat, the ancient gods are characterised by sorrow, fear and dismay. Saturn is depicted in a state of immobility indicative of the loss of power:

> Upon the sodden ground
> His old right hand lay nerveless, listless, dead,
> Unsceptred; and his realmless eyes were closed;
> While his bowed head seemed listening to the Earth,
> His ancient mother, for some comfort yet.
> (*Hyperion*, I, ll. 17–21)

As they voice their pain, we begin to realise that this, too, is a poem of metamorphosis: these gods are undergoing a loss which would be termed a 'fall' within a Christian narrative like *Paradise Lost*. And in keeping with its close affinity to the first two books of Milton's poem, the first two books of *Hyperion* deal with the aftermath of a war in heaven and the rousing possibility of a hero who, though diminished, refuses to accede to the narrative in which he finds himself. Hyperion is very much Keats's rewriting of Milton's Satan, the rousing, indefatigable leader of the rebel angels after their crushing and damning defeat.

In their fall from power, the Titans become strangely knowable from a human perspective and Keats draws this to our attention with a self-conscious use of a well-established form of epic comparison between the great and the small, the supernatural and the merely human. At the opening of the poem, the Titan leader Saturn is comforted by Thea, wife of Hyperion, and, as she prepares for her speech, our attention is drawn to the strange difference between god and mortal: 'One hand she pressed upon that aching spot / Where beats the human heart, as if just there, / Though an immortal, she felt cruel pain.'[15] The condition of our humanity, as so often in Keats, is measured by this insistence upon aching pain. The significance of the change now affecting the Titans is further revealed in Saturn's response to Thea when he describes himself as alienated: 'I am gone / Away from my own bosom; I have left / My strong identity, my real self' (*H*, I, ll. 112–14). In charting the terrible fall of the Titans from their position of power, Keats is also defining a shift in the nature of identity. The new order to be brought in by Apollo will also involve a new kind of subjectivity. Here Titanic selfhood is characterised by singleness and strength. The shock to the psyche of Saturn arrives in the very appearance of a fissure in what hitherto has been a confirmedly homogeneous selfhood where self, power, position and external reality exist in absolute integration with each other. With defeat comes change, instability and plurality.

The perilous doom of the new situation (which parallels that of the exiled fallen angels in *Paradise Lost*) is felt palpably by the hero. We are told that 'horrors, portioned to a giant nerve / Oft made Hyperion ache' (*H*, I, ll. 175–6). The new cosmic order is typically registered by Keats in physiological terms, here in the form of a suitably epic 'giant nerve'. As yet, still retaining his sublime radiance as 'blazing Hyperion', the hero is now distraught that 'his eternal essence' is able to recognise spectres of pain, horrors and monstrous forms. His new affinity or kinship with such forms – like Satan's with Sin and Death in *Paradise Lost* – turns out to be more self-defining than he could imagine. After his rousing response to the defeated troops, he retains a strange undetermined sense of dread. His legions 'Bestirred themselves, thrice horrible and cold; / And from the mirrored level where he stood / A mist arose, as from a scummy marsh' (*H*, I, ll. 256–8). In such a mirroring, Hyperion senses a diminished version of his former blazing selfhood. Keats confirms the level of monstrous transformation in the god's unconscious reaction to his changed status: 'At this, through all his bulk an agony / Crept gradual, from the feet unto the crown, / Like a lithe serpent vast and muscular / Making slow way, with head and neck convulsed / From over-strainèd might' (*H*, I, ll. 259–63).

Not only is the fiery Titan god diminished through his affiliation with 'Pale phantoms' and the 'scummy marsh' (both reminiscent of 'La Belle Dame sans Merci'),[16] but his very identity is beginning to

operate on multiple levels. Keats's description of his agony extends
this as it offers his reader the image of Hyperion's other monstrous
self, with its affinity to the uncanny serpent/woman of 'Lamia'.
Instead of ethereal radiance, we are provided with a figure of gross
corporeality. In similar fashion, book II of *Hyperion* opens with the
fallen Titans condemned and confined in their new element,
'Locked up like veins of metal, cramped and screwed; / Without a
motion, save of their big hearts / Heaving in pain, and horribly
convulsed / With sanguine feverous boiling gurge of pulse' (*H*, II,
ll. 25–8). Just as Lamia receives her woman's body 'convulsed with
scarlet pain', here the ancient gods fall into a pulsing corporeality
horribly proximate to humanity.

   Set against the Satanic sublime of 'blazing Hyperion' now rup-
tured with a contending self of monstrous corporeality is Keats's
vision of Apollo. What we have of the uncompleted poem ends
with the new sun god's fascinatingly painful metamorphosis and
the promotion of a radically different conception of the self. In
what there is of book III of *Hyperion* we quickly leave the woeful
Titans behind in order to concentrate on the youthful Apollo who
wanders forth on a new pastoral morning in a state of tearful
response to the 'murmurous noise of waves' (*H*, III, l. 40). He soon
encounters an unknown, but uncannily familiar goddess who fills
him with perplexity. She explains that she has 'forsaken old and
sacred thrones / For prophecies' of him, and he immediately identifies her as Mnemosyne (goddess of memory and mother of the
muses) as he finds himself articulating her name. As she remains
mute, he reads 'A wondrous lesson in [her] silent face'. His 'aching
ignorance' is now replaced by divine wisdom as he is translated
into a god in an act of unconscious transference:

> Knowledge enormous makes a God of me.
> Names, deeds, grey legends, dire events, rebellions,
> Majesties, sovran voices, agonies,
> Creations and destroyings, all at once
> Pour into the wide hollows of my brain,
> And deify me, as if some blithe wine
> Or bright elixir peerless I had drunk,
> And so become immortal.
> (*Hyperion*, III, ll. 113–20)

What had been the oppressive weight of history in book III of
Endymion is here the celebrated stuff of creativity passed between

goddess and youth and, on a wider level, between historical epochs – between Titans and the new order of the Olympian gods.

In Keats's imagining of such historical change, Mnemosyne acts as female go-between. The youthful Apollo gives himself up to her content – the accumulated wisdom of ages – in an act of radical feminisation. The ecstatic metamorphosis which follows is very different from the flaming masculine energy and determined, fixed identity of Hyperion. In this process of historical change the flow or exchange of creativity depends upon a loss of identity and what is tantamount to possession of the self by another. And the terms of this metamorphosis eerily prefigure those of the female Lamia in Keats's later narrative poem of that name. Like hers, Apollo's achievement of a new identity is founded on loss and pain and culminates in an eerie shriek. Unfortunately, the poem ends before we know what transformation Keats has in store for his young god on a more corporeal level:

> Soon wild commotions shook him, and made flush
> All the immortal fairness of his limbs –
> Most like the struggle at the gate of death;
> Or liker still to one who should take leave
> Of pale immortal death, and with a pang
> As hot as death's is chill, with fierce convulse
> Die into life: so young Apollo anguished.
> His very hair, his golden tresses famed
> Kept undulation round his eager neck.
> During the pain Mnemosyne upheld
> Her arms as one who prophesied. – At length
> Apollo shrieked – and lo! From all his limbs
> Celestial ...
>
> (*Hyperion*, III, ll. 124–37)

Leigh Hunt was obviously disturbed by this ending to Keats's epic project. In the 'deification of Apollo' he found 'something too effeminate and human in the way in which Apollo receives the exaltation which his wisdom is giving him. He weeps and wonders somewhat too fondly; but his powers gather nobly on him as he proceeds.'[17] Unfortunately, he too fails to offer any further commentary on the shriek. Undoubtedly, even an admirer such as Hunt (whose own predilection for the excesses of the fancy was the butt of his literary and political opponents) finds it difficult to fully endorse the pivotal moment of Keats's uncompleted epic. Instead of heroic action or resolve, epitomised by Satan and Hyperion as well as earlier classical military heroes, Keats's heroism appears to take a peculiarly passive and uncontrollable form. Rather than determined self-autonomy in the manner of some of Byron's heroes such as Manfred (himself a humanist recreation of Milton's Satan), Keats provides us with a Bacchic ecstasy in which the self, represented through the body, is merely the vehicle through which knowledge passes in the form of pain and sorrow. The poem ends with a spectacular moment of transformation, but the heroic self on offer – at least at this point – is anything but that of the 'foreseeing God' capable of 'shaping his own action' whom Keats refers to in his letters.

III. *THE FALL OF HYPERION*

Keats returned to an epic Miltonic mode and to the same body of mythological material when he began work in July 1819 on *The Fall of Hyperion. A Dream*. Like *Hyperion*, it remained uncompleted. The fall of the Titans is here recounted by Moneta – another version of the goddess of memory Mnemosyne who had figured so prominently in the earlier poem. Keats also returns to the mode of dream-vision as a means of defining the nature and the limits of the poem. *The Fall of Hyperion* opens with an anxious and severe questioning of the role and efficacy of the poet. In the very first paragraph, the speaker/poet immediately questions the relationship between dreaming and poetry: something central to Keats's own early ideas of creativity and to which he gave creative and articulate form in his poem 'Sleep and Poetry'. Here, in his epic, the degree of his profound scepticism and self-doubt is evident in the poem's opening gambit: 'Fanatics have their dreams.' The poem's opening paragraph turns out to be a radical self-questioning which immediately places a frame of qualification around the dream-vision which forms the body of the poem. If the challenge to the figure of the poet comes from the fanatic at one end of the spectrum, it comes from ordinary human experience at the other. The poem's scepticism is allied to its strongly developed sense of democratic spirit:

> Who alive can say,
> 'Thou art no Poet – mayst not tell thy dreams'?
> Since every man whose soul is not a clod

> Hath visions, and would speak, if he had loved,
> And been well nurtured in his mother tongue.
> Whether the dream now purposed to rehearse
> Be Poet's or Fanatic's will be known
> When this warm scribe my hand is in the grave.
>   (*Fall of Hyperion*, I, ll. 11–18)

Within the dream-vision and the encounter with the initially unidentified Moneta, the poet is led to an altar and in ascending its steps finds himself threatened with mortality. But he is allowed to survive only to realise that he has been spared on the grounds of his 'unworthiness' – and not for his transcendent or immortal qualities as a poet. Rather than a poet, he is a mere dreamer.

The Fall of Hyperion begins, then, with a series of fraught definitions of the role of the poet in relation to ordinariness and the visionary which centre on the nature of human suffering. In response to the poet's request to 'purge off' his 'mind's film'[18] Moneta responds with the following chastening revelation:

> [...] 'None can usurp this height,' returned that shade,
> 'But those to whom the miseries of the world
> Are misery, and will not let them rest.
> All else who find a haven in the world,
> Where they may thoughtless sleep away their days,
> If by a chance into this fane they come,
> Rot on the pavement where thou rotted'st half.'
>   (*Fall of Hyperion*, I, ll. 147–53)

The poet's response to this correlation of suffering with vision, truth and knowledge is, as one might expect from Keats, to turn to the power of love – and love manifest in philanthropic actions:

> 'Are there not thousands in the world,' said I,
> Encouraged by the sooth voice of the shade,
> 'Who love their fellows even to the death;
> Who feel the giant agony of the world;
> And more, like slaves to poor humanity,
> Labour for mortal good? I sure should see
> Other men here: but I am here alone.'
>   (*Fall of Hyperion*, I, ll. 154–60)

Unfortunately for the poet, he has once again mistaken the categories and Moneta's response subjects him to a severe process of definition:

> 'They are no dreamers weak,
> They seek no wonder but the human face;
> No music but a happy-noted voice –
> They come not here, they have no thought to come –
> And thou art here, for thou art less than they –
> What benefit canst thou, or all thy tribe,
> To the great world? Thou art a dreaming thing,
> A fever of thyself. Think of the Earth;
> What bliss even in hope is there for thee?
> What haven? Every creature hath its home;
> Every sole man hath days of joy and pain,
> Whether his labours be sublime or low –
> The pain alone; the joy alone; distinct:'
>   (*Fall of Hyperion*, I, ll. 162–74)

Devastating though this is to the poet, it also confirms him as an alienated, isolated figure suffering apart in his crisis of identity and existential angst, aside from the mainstream. But his informative exchanges with Moneta proceed to home in on the relationship between the poet and social usefulness. Distraught at being described as unworthy, the speaker/poet begins to question poetry more generally: 'sure not all / Those melodies sung into the world's ear / Are useless; sure a poet is a sage, / A humanist, physician to all men.'[19] In radical conflict with the very form and conception of the poem comes the response from the goddess that 'The poet and the dreamer are distinct'. Our poet, mistaken in his idealism, falls into the latter, lesser, category which leads him, in desperation, to cry out against 'Apollo! Faded, far-flown Apollo!'.[20] Given Keats's own worship of Apollo, this is self-critique of a high order. Having been severely chastened, even redefined, the poet asks Moneta to define herself and tell her story which is to be the main body of the poem. The final and significant act in this frame to the epic narrative consists in Moneta granting his wish on the grounds of his 'goodwill' and the poem proceeds in terms of the same kind of transference of vast knowledge which took place between Mnemosyne and Apollo in *Hyperion*.

In many ways, this accommodation of the poet's lack of worth stands in significant opposition to the apotheosis of Apollo we examined in *Hyperion*. Unworthy though he is claimed to be, the poet receives the cursed knowledge of Moneta and, in doing so, the burden of that knowledge is transformed to 'wonder'. Despite all the questioning, a metamorphosis is still to take place. The dreamer is to receive his dream vision – the story of the fall of the ancient gods:

> 'The sacrifice is done, but not the less
> Will I be kind to thee for thy goodwill.
> My power, which to me is still a curse,
> Shall be to thee a wonder; for the scenes
> Still swooning vivid through my globèd brain,
> With an electrical changing misery,
> Thou shalt with those dull mortal eyes behold,
> Free from all pain, if wonder pain thee not.'
> (*Fall of Hyperion*, I, ll. 241–8)

On these distinctly mixed and ambivalent terms, the unworthy dreamer-poet joins with the 'forlorn divinity' of a 'withered race'. This is no ecstatic metamorphosis. Even the word 'wonder' is immediately accompanied by a recognition of possible pain and is already qualified by the reality of 'dull mortal eyes'. There's an unspectacular power of kind mutuality at work here. Both sides share in the burden of loss and suffering which lives in the shadow of the knowledge of ordinary human mortality. Keats's epic project attaches itself to a peculiarly remote and failed heroism in order to reorientate poetry's connection with humanity. His epic abstractions are focused on the truth which lies in the suffering of ordinary experience, not in the artificial yearnings of the poet dreamer.

Keats, then, turns his back on the stark Miltonic epic mode of his two Hyperion poems. The sublime austerity he had earlier relished in anticipation of writing the first Hyperion poem and which he had described as a 'naked' and 'Grecian manner' was now, in September 1819, no longer to his taste. He began to see it negatively. Instead of authorising a line of epic poetry, Milton's specialised and often Latinate blank verse now seems to him an idiosyncratic or, at least, unique production, a foreign and artificial imposition upon the language which should hold little attraction for future writers concerned for the purity of diction of their mother tongue. In a famous letter to his friend John Hamilton Reynolds, dated 21 September and often read in conjunction with his ode 'To Autumn', Keats reveals his reasons for having 'given up' on *The Fall of Hyperion*:

> I always somehow associate Chatterton with autumn. He is the purest writer in the English Language. He has no French idiom, or

particles like Chaucer<s> – 'tis genuine English Idiom in English words. I have given up Hyperion – there were too many Miltonic inversions in it – Miltonic verse cannot be written but in an artful or rather artist's humour. I wish to give myself up to other sensations. English ought to be kept up. It may be interesting to you to pick out some lines from Hyperion and put a mark x to the false beauty proceeding from art, and the one ‖ to the true voice of feeling. Upon my soul 'twas imagination I cannot make the distinction – Every now & then there is a Miltonic intonation – But I cannot make the division properly. (*Letters*, II, 167)

Three days later he wrote to his brother George along the same lines. Here Chatterton, the dedicatee of his poetical romance *Endymion*, is once again the measure of poetic linguistic purity. And if there was a suspicion in the letter to Reynolds of his own work being infected by the foreign artifice of Milton's verse, here Keats moves further towards a shuddering revulsion towards his former model:

I shall never become attach'd to a foreign idiom so as to put it into my writings. The Paradise lost though so fine in itself is a curruption of our Language – it should be kept as it is unique – a curiosity. a beautiful and grand Curiosity. The most remarkable Production of the world – A northern dialect accommodating itself to greek and latin inversions and intonations. The purest english, I think – or what ought to be the purest – is Chatterton's – The Language had existed long enough to be entirely uncorrupted of Chaucer's gallicisms and still the old words are used – Chatterton's language is entirely northern – I prefer the native music of it to Milton's cut by feet I have but lately stood on my guard against Milton. Life to him would be death to me. Miltonic verse cannot be written but it the vein of art – I wish to devote myself to another sensation –
(*Letters*, II, 212)

The contrast between 'native music' and 'Milton's cut by feet' is telling. 'Cut by feet' captures his sense of Milton's deliberate, even painful, labour in the service of an artificial monumentalism. The final blow comes on another, altogether more metaphysical level with the declaration that: 'Life to him would be death to me.'

The strength of this reaction is all the more revealing given Keats's seeming immersion in all things Miltonic only a month before. Setting himself to write the second attempt at the Hyperion mythology Keats is buoyed by the thrill of poetic ambition and the

dedication of himself to the task ahead, and he writes to Reynolds
in a high pitch of creative excitement:

> The more I know what my diligence may in time probably effect; the
> more does my heart distend with Pride and Obstinacy – I feel it in
> my power to become a popular writer – I feel it in my strength to
> refuse the poisonous suffrage of a public – My own being which I
> know to be becomes of more consequence to me than the crowds of
> Shadows in the Shape of Man and women that inhabit a kingdom.
> The Soul is a world of itself and has enough to do in its own home –
> Those whom I know already and who have grown as it were a part
> of myself I could not do without: but for the rest of Mankind they
> are as much a dream to me as Miltons Hierarchies [...] I have noth-
> ing to speak of but myself – and what can I say but what I feel? If
> you should have any reason to regret this state of excitement in me,
> I will turn the tide of your feelings in the right channel by mention-
> ing that it is the only state for the best sort of Poetry – that is all I
> care for, all I live for.   (*Letters*, II, 146–7)

Even in describing the state of his heart, Keats invests himself in the
language of Milton's Satan and the whole passage is suffused with
a self-conscious egotism which never quite raises itself to a level of
self-critique. Dedication to the act of composition is sufficient legit-
imation and justification, it seems. The terms in which he fashions
his self-image as poet here sit uneasily alongside the attack on the
self-involved poet as dreamer which dominates the opening of the
poem he was about to produce from that very state of creativity.
Equally, the claimed confidence in his 'power to become a popular
writer' sits problematically next to his seeming disdain for the 'poi-
sonous suffrage of a public'. The dangers of the claim that 'the Soul
is a world of itself' would soon be met by the counter-claims of a
suffering humanity and the mysterious truth or meaning to be
found in such suffering.

Keats's abortive Miltonic epics enable him to explore the historical and metaphysical implications of love and to redefine his sense
of the utility of the poet. At the same time as he examines love as
the mediatory power which links us with the divine, he finds himself fulfilling the highest epic function of the poet, but sees himself
moving further away from the very stuff of humanity. The problems besetting him in *Hyperion* and *The Fall of Hyperion* are those
of Milton (particularly in the figure of Satan) writ large: to write
about human passion and psychology with regard to those who are

not (quite) human. In the next chapter, in his famous narrative poems, Keats's exploration of romance is never in danger of losing contact with human passion, though it is as firmly focused on the problem of history and the prevailing commercial spirit of the age.

3

Narrating Romance: 'Isabella', 'La Belle Dame sans Merci', 'The Eve of St Agnes', and 'Lamia'

'Isabella; or the Pot of Basil', 'The Eve of St Agnes' and 'Lamia' represent Keats's most concerted and, in some ways, most disturbing development of poetic romance.[1] In these narratives, it is possible to observe a progressive toughening of his idea of romantic love directed to a male audience. This involves an increasing level of authorial distancing and studied objectivity which often works in tandem with a creative use of historical difference. In all these poems, including the short ballad 'La Belle Dame sans Merci', Keats manipulates the historical perspective in order to frame his representation of human passion. In these poems, romantic love is defined by the threat which surrounds it – whether it be the murderous violence of the brothers in 'Isabella', the mysterious malaise of the knight and the doubting voices which surround him in 'La Belle Dame sans Merci', the violent, animalistic 'foemen' of the 'Eve of St Agnes', or the destroying knowledge of Apollonius in 'Lamia'. In all, cruelty plays a key role, not only in this process of differentiation to provide a sense of romance under siege, but as an integral aspect of the erotically charged aesthetic. The idea of romance precariously situated in an uncongenial, threatening society mixes easily with a fantasy of pain. In the narratives, there is a complex, at times sensational, mixing of pleasure with pain. It is in this respect that Keats might be said to be reinforcing the masculine identity of his version of poetic romance. His own uncertainties about 'Isabella' centred on its knowingness, particularly its sexual knowingness, and how this might make him vulnerable to mockery as well as critique. To this end, he set about toughening up his romance by making it more objective – less recognisable as the projection of its author. At the same time, these romance narratives creatively dramatise the question of sexual knowledge. The ending of 'Lamia' – with its staging of a face-to-face show-down of competing knowledges – is, in this respect, the fitting culmination of Keats's daring exploration of the meaning of desire.

I. 'ISABELLA'

'Isabella; or the Pot of Basil' was written as part of a project undertaken with friend and fellow poet John Hamilton Reynolds in the spring of 1818. The plan to compose a set of verse narratives based on Boccaccio's *Decameron* (c.1351) was never completed and Keats remained unconvinced by the one poem he had managed to produce. In conversation with Richard Woodhouse nearly eighteen months later, he still considered it too vulnerable to be published. According to his friend, 'he could not bear [it] ... now. It appeared to him mawkish' (*Letters*, II, 162). 'Mawkishness' or falling into sickly, false or feeble sentiment was something of which, most famously, Byron was to accuse Keats. Woodhouse's immediate response is to defend 'Isabella' from such a charge and to deflect criticism onto the mood of unprepared or unsympathetic readers, claiming that '[t]he feeling of mawkishness [...] comes upon us where any thing of great tenderness & excessive simplicity is met with when we are not in a sufficiently tender & simple frame of mind to bear it'. There was not, he assured his friend and Keats's publisher John Taylor, anything in the 'most passionate parts of Isabella to excite this feeling' of 'revulsion, or resiliency' (*Letters*, II, 162). In a letter to Woodhouse dated only two days after this account, Keats explains that there is 'too much inexperience of live, and simplicity of knowledge in it'; it was simply, he confessed, 'too smokeable' (*Letters*, II, 174). To 'smoke', as in 'to make fun of, to jeer at; to ridicule, banter, or quiz', belongs to the language of eighteenth-century cant deployed by young men about town. Keats uses the word on a good number of occasions in his letters where he and his friends are the ones doing the 'smoking'. His sensitivity in this instance to being the one laughed at is interesting for the way it is expressed in the terms of his homosocially bonded group. It suggests that the poem's vulnerability might also lie in its lack of sexual knowingness: that it might be too revealing of its author's own ignorance. Significantly, Keats doesn't use the more positive term 'innocence' to describe – or defend – this vulnerability; the poem's 'inexperience' and 'simplicity' are not qualities he is willing to defend, but more like stages in a process of maturation which must be left behind. He is alert to the position of a reviewer who might find an 'amusing sober-sadness' about it and admits that, in such a position, he might 'quiz' it himself. He now realises he must treat the reading public with more 'finesse', by which we might understand not only greater sophistication, but more strategic specialisation. With hindsight, he is able to discern a development from 'Isabella' through the other two major narrative poems: 'There is no objection of this kind to Lamia – A good deal to St Agnes' Eve – only not so glaring' (*Letters*, II, 174). The trajectory is also, one might add, characterised by increasing sexual knowingness.

Responses were mixed. Charles Lamb thought 'Isabella' 'the finest thing' and a reviewer in the *New Monthly Magazine* praised its 'naked and affecting simplicity which goes straight to the heart', though he concedes it 'has not the luxury of description, nor the rich love-scenes' of Barry Cornwall's *A Sicilian Story*.[2] Keats's own misgivings about 'Isabella' and the mixed response of readers and reviewers point to a precariousness of taste, particularly in relation to romance and its representation of sexuality. In particular, there's an anxiety here about the degree of knowledge which such a narrative romance might reveal in its author as well as in its characters. This, in turn, raises questions about the audience: its politeness and its gender composition. Keats's declaration of intent to go for more 'finesse' as far as audience is concerned might be seen as pushing him further towards an exclusively male readership. In many ways, this fraught conjunction of heartfelt simplicity and sexual knowingness is a resurfacing of a familiar issue at the heart of the literature of sensibility, most famously exploited for comic effect by Laurence Sterne in *A Sentimental Journey* (1768) where sentiment is self-consciously caught between authentic feeling and *double entendre*. The problem for Keats seems to be that he is situated somewhere in the middle of this uncertainty of taste. To write about the simplicity of romantic passion is likely to subject him to ridicule; to include the erotic alongside the sentimental risks confusion. The way ahead might be to push more definitively towards a more robust, masculinised version of romance.

Reynolds published his own attempts in a volume entitled *The Garden of Florence and Other Poems* (1821)[3] where he lamented the untimely death of his friend and announced his own imminent withdrawal from a poetic career for the more financially secure offices of the legal profession. The protagonists in his 'Ladye of Provence' are described in terms which reflect the shared enterprise of the original project with Keats: 'They were as brothers in their sports, – their joys, / Their wonted occupations', and the dedication humourously expresses his wish to give up 'drawling verses for drawing leases',[4] as if the process is one of maturation: the young man leaving the romance of poetry behind for financial security. This conflict between the romance of poetry and actual romance is given more extended treatment in the introduction where it becomes further entangled with the knowledge of Keats's own short life:

> Thou hast entreated me 'to write no more',
>   To turn aside from the consuming art;
> And can I shun the voice that I adore,
>   The voice that hath an echo in my heart?
> Perchance a gentleman of twenty-four,
>   And *upwards*, should abandon verse in part,
> And keep a house, and plunge in tax vexations,
> And die, and leave a will for his relations.[5]

Such a stark confession would seem to confirm Donald Reiman's devastating claim that 'Reynolds's self-doubt is both the unstated subject and the fatal flaw of much of his work',[6] but the strange mixture of conflicting possibilities here is revealing of the degree to which the Boccaccio project was caught up in a very particular contest between the competing forces of poetry, money and romance in the case of both poets. Even more revealing, perhaps, for our understanding of Keats, is the correlation made here between poetry and romance: that poetry is a kind of romance and that both – in their different ways – are 'consuming'. The process of maturing and becoming a man, more particularly a 'gentleman', is at the forefront of Reynolds's anxieties. Poetry and romance both provide threats to such an idea; in both, the young man faces the possibility of wasting his energies by being consumed by the object of his desire, be that a female lover or the demon poesy. Reynolds's retrospective gloss on his own contributions to the Boccaccio project provides a useful point of comparison to Keats in terms of the way it considers the possibility and impossibility of poetic ambition within the confines of middle-class financial security and the domestic arrangements necessary for marriage.

In the two poems themselves, 'The Garden of Florence' and 'The Ladye of Provence', Reynolds presents his heroines in such a way as to remove them from an active role in sexual passion, although in other works he represents the dangerously debilitating power of heterosexual passion through haunting *femmes fatales*. The gross appetitive desire of both stories manifests itself in a grotesque culmination of the narrative, particularly in the case of 'The Lady of Provence' where the heroine is duped into eating the cooked heart of her lover. This serves to detract from the transgressive nature of her desire by transposing it to another form of appetite. In a narrative climax which might have appealed to Keats, the heroine Indreana suffers the following disturbing news about her lover before throwing herself to her death:

> 'Tis Gardastagno's heart thou hast devour'd!
> These hands did gather it – I knew 'twould pleasure
> Thy most depraved fancy and false taste!
> His heart's torn casket lieth in the wood, –
> The heart itself thy body hath inurn'd![7]

Love or desire is here saved and sanitised by its separation from the grotesque body. Such unknowing passivity lies at the other end of the spectrum to Keats's sensationalism in the 'Eve of St Agnes' and in 'Lamia' where the narrative depends most definitely on the sexual knowingness and proficiency of its ambivalent heroine. In the case of 'Isabella; or the Pot of Basil' there's a strong likelihood, not least because of the precariousness of such transpositions of appetite, that the claims of 'depraved fancy' and 'false taste' here ascribed to the heroine of Reynolds's narrative might transfer themselves to the author.

Keats's narrative romance clearly sets itself against the world of commerce. Isabella's story might well have engendered an exploration of familial schism, with her two brothers responsible for the death of her lover Lorenzo. We might have been introduced to a domestic psychological conflict. Instead, Keats chooses to develop the brothers as a sign of money-making to set against that of romantic love. At one point, they are even described simply as 'money-bags'. The poem first enters into a world of violence when it describes their 'torched mines' and 'noisy factories' almost as if they are institutions of slavery: 'And many once proud-quivered loins did melt / In blood from stinging whip' ('Isabella', ll. 109–10). The contemporary resonance slavery might have for Keats's audience is then extended with a description in the next stanza of imperialism's barely comprehended reach into lives of subject peoples and the realm of nature:

> For them the Ceylon diver held his breath,
>   And went all naked to the hungry shark;
> For them his ears gushed blood; for them in death
>   The seal on the cold ice with piteous bark
> Lay full of darts; for them alone did seethe
>   A thousand men in troubles wide and dark:
> Half-ignorant, they turned an easy wheel,
> That set sharp racks at work to pinch and peel.
>   ('Isabella', XV, ll. 113–20)

Just as Keats's poem demonstrates the projective power of its exoticising imagination by imaging the felt interiority of remote suffering, it defines the murderous brothers (or 'ledger-men' as it calls them at this point) as 'self-retired' in their commercial pride. And it is this uncanny power of vision, the reach of their commercialism, which brings them the knowledge of Isabella's love for Lorenzo. The hostile world in which Keats sets his version of the story, as well as his motivation for love's destruction, is, then, interestingly moved beyond the limits of family and family psychology; it is clearly defined more generally as a societal, cultural problem about prevailing values of wealth and the organisation of labour. Before proceeding to the gory Gothic heart of his narrative, Keats cleverly defines a dominant and pervasive commercial spirit which is both cruel and exploitative, even one might suggest, given the last line of the stanza quoted above, verging on the sadistic and, at one level at least, his imagination goes out to this negative side of the poem.[8]

Even before Keats's decision to set off his story of bloody romance in a hostile commercial world, however, he introduces his own disturbingly mixed and paradoxical idea of pleasure into the equation with the concluding couplet to stanza XIII: 'Even bees, the little almsmen of spring-bowers, / Know there is richest juice in poison-flowers' (XIII, ll. 103–4). In a characteristic moment of self-reflection when the poem speaks, as it often does, to its self-conscious remaking of old romance, Keats introduces his own disturbing combination of romance and annihilation. It is also a transitional moment in the poem when we switch from a consideration of the lovers' happiness to the pleasure experienced by the narrator and reader in, respectively, the telling or reading of romance. At such a moment, Keats enacts the poem's at once exciting and disturbing capacity for objectification – or commodification, if we relate it to the economic fantasy of the poem. We are suddenly removed from a sympathetic or empathetic consideration of the young lovers and asked to consider them as victims of a mode of storytelling. Attached to his sensuous and sympathetic rendering of events and passions is a removed, playful, even cruel, narrative pleasure.

Part of this disturbing process of objectification derives from Keats's historical self-consciousness, manifest most obviously as an elegaic tribute to Boccaccio in stanzas XIX and XX where he begins by addressing 'O eloquent and famed Boccaccio!', but soon begins to stress the pastness of the Italian's existence: 'And of thy lilies, that do paler grow / Now they can no more hear thy gittern's tune' (XIX, ll. 145, 149–50). Keats clearly has a strong sense of the deathly nature of the text he's reworking. Even the honouring of Boccaccio in stanza XX takes the form of greeting his 'gone spirit'. There's clearly a troubled sense of propriety at work here, with Keats struggling to observe a pious regard for the past, registered in his recognition to 'move on soberly, as it is meet', at the same time as offering an apology for 'venturing syllables that ill beseem / The quiet glooms of such a piteous theme' (ll. 154, 151–2). This disturbance reaches a climax as the poem moves to the gory denouement of Isabella's sad tale. At the point where she visits the spot in the forest where her lover's corpse lies buried, Keats begins to mix the old romance with his own disturbing brand of sensuously perceived detail. After finding Lorenzo's 'soiled glove' Isabella 'put[s] it in her bosom, where it dries / And freezes utterly unto the bone / Those dainties made to still an infant's cries' (XLVII, ll. 373–4). For the modern reader, Keats's euphemistic description of breasts is embarrassing in its own right, but, coupled with the graphic description of an act brought on by – at this stage – a pathological response to her lover's death, it is even more disconcerting. The abrupt combination of explicitness and coyness appears unhelpfully awkward. Yet this combination might be said to be entirely characteristic of the kind of passion Keats is exploring in this particular narrative. Early on in the poem, the passion between the lovers is represented as a consuming illness, more particularly a fever which, unless assuaged by a sweating or open manifestation in the form of a declaration or reciprocation with the beloved, will inevitably lead to death. Passion here, as often in romance, is synonymous with death and disease. Keats is also alert to the power of this passion in his particularly medically informed way which tends to focus on the circulation of the blood. This is particularly pertinent to the case of young Lorenzo who finds himself suddenly diminished by the fever fit of passion to the extent that:

> His heart beat awfully against his side;
> And to his heart he inwardly did pray
> For power to speak; but still the ruddy tide
> Stifled his voice, and pulsed resolve away –
> ('Isabella', VI, ll. 42–5)

The poem's young hero finds himself unmanned by romance manifested most graphically by increased blood pressure. The resulting diminished sense of masculine identity is something which Keats captures well in the stanza's concluding couplet: 'Yet brought him to the meekness of a child: /Alas! when passion is both meek and wild!' This uncanny combination of 'meek and wild' where we might more usually expect 'meek and mild' constitutes the difficult and unstable territory of the whole poem which, on the meek side, leans towards 'mawkishness' or feeble sentimentality and, on the other, pushes towards gothic sensationalism.

As if to draw attention to the problem, Keats breaks into the narrative after the incident with the soiled glove. The terms in which he does so point to the difficulty of rewriting this old romance and the tensions within his own current version of it. There's a strong suggestion here that Keats is, in mid-creation, rethinking his own take on romance, of how a contemporary, early nineteenth-century romance might operate as well as how it might challenge the propriety of established good taste:

> Ah! wherefore all this wormy circumstance?
> Why linger at the yawning tomb so long?

O for the gentleness of old Romance,
  The simple plaining of a minstrel's song!
Fair reader, at the old tale take a glance,
  For here, in truth, it doth not well belong
To speak – O turn thee to the very tale,
And taste the music of that vision pale.
                    ('Isabella', XLIX, ll. 385–92)

Rather than an apology, this stanza might be read as an aggressive statement of intent – Keats committing himself to the more dangerous territory of 'wormy circumstance'. What seems like a nostalgic hankering after 'the gentleness of old Romance' and the simplicity of the past, turns out to be a way of directing the female reader ('fair readers' in this period are usually presumed to be women) to the less disturbing original. In this context, Keats's conjuring of the provocative phrase 'wormy circumstance' might rightly be considered risqué. He's clearly intent here on rewriting romance in a manner which is more likely to suit a male reader. In addition to the gender particularity of Keats's self-consciousness, there's also a historical dimension to his sense of the difference between old and new romance: a belief that the past represents an unrecoverable simplicity, the present a haunted complexity in which romance and romance narrative might struggle to survive. The markers of modernity with which the murderous brothers are represented clearly signal this larger problem: a culture whose economic dynamic militates against romance. 'Romance' is itself, of course, a sign of the historically defined, even superannuated, by the time that Keats is writing.

Having interrupted his narrative in the middle of its gory denouement in order to draw attention in this way to his own still forming sense of romance, Keats resumes in order to deliver what remains as the most disturbed and disturbing aspect of the poem: Isabella's recovery of the head of her dead lover; her preparation of it before burying it in the pot of basil; and her continued watering of the fragrant plant with her tears. Of these, the stanza detailing the preparation of Lorenzo's head is still, probably, the most unnerving and embarrassing for many contemporary readers:

In anxious secrecy they took it home,
  And then the prize was all for Isabel.
She calmed its wild hair with a golden comb,
  And all around each eye's sepulchral cell

Pointed each fringed lash; the smeared loam
  With tears, as chilly as a dripping well,
She drenched away – and still she combed, and kept
Sighing all day – and still she kissed, and wept.
                              ('Isabella', LI, ll. 401–8)

Faced with such pathological detail many readers will immediately consign this part of the poem to the category ludicrous. There's something deeply unsettling about Isabella's activity here, and not simply because it strains the credibility of a forensically informed imagination. It is, for one thing, horribly reminiscent of a girl's grooming of her doll, right down to the straightening of the eyelashes. Romance ends in a deranged grief which infantilises both lovers: she a girl with her favourite toy, he a manikin. Romance, which we might equate with a maturation process, in this tragic, agonised form, returns to childhood and within that, the child's stymied repetitions of transfixed play. Isabella's lot is to be consigned to a grief-stricken immobility from which she is released only when her brothers take her fetish away from her, though even here the repeated refrain which ends the poem – 'O cruelty, / To steal my basil-pot away from me' (ll. 503–4) – serves as a reminder of her fixation. In many ways, this much maligned and dismissed ending to the poem does, at least, perform a fitting close to a narrative whose main passion, as we have seen, is an unhappy combination of the 'meek and wild': mawkishness and 'wormy circumstance'.

II. 'LA BELLE DAME SANS MERCI'

Keats's 'La Belle Dame sans Merci: a Ballad' has generated a considerable amount of critical debate for such a short poem. The inclusion of the word 'ballad' in its title immediately raises questions about excess in relation to Keats's idea of romance. It appears to be surplus to requirements: an unnecessary supplement. In the same mode, the original publication of the poem in Leigh Hunt's *Indicator* included the pseudonym 'Caviare', suggesting the poet's relish for an indication of self-conscious aesthetic gusto. And in its representation of suffering chivalric masculinity at the hands of a bewitching form of femininity Keats also immediately created something of an icon for the coming Victorian age; the poem became a favourite source of inspiration for the pre-Raphaelites.

More recent critical commentaries have focused on the problem
of cause and effect in the poem, the difficulty of deciding who is
speaking, and, of course, the meaning of the knight's apparent
malaise. The poem begins with an unidentified speaker immediately diagnosing and interrogating the 'knight-at-arms'. From the
outset, those last two words 'at-arms' seem strangely redundant.
Here is a knight removed from the more obviously dangerous and
masculine territory of war, but, as we soon find out, located in a
scene of nature with a story of encounter to relate which concerns
itself with the differently risky business of chivalry and romance.
Even at this stage, it's apparent that the poem's playful fascination
with excess also takes the form of multiplying perspectives and repetitions. We encounter a speaker encountering a knight who tells us
of his encounter with a bewitching beauty. This very deliberate lay-
ering is related to the poem's historical self-consciousness, its rather
arch deployment of medievalism, probably encouraged through
Keats's reading of Coleridge's 'The Rime of the Ancient Mariner'
and 'Christabel'. History, too, is drawn to our attention by this lay-
ering. Keats signals the difference and distance of history as well as
its seeming artificiality by this multiplying of perspective. This is
something which Keats also uses to great effect in 'The Eve of
St Agnes' where he surrounds the passionate narrative of the poem
with a deathly frame which serves as a powerful reminder to the
reader of the way in which, in his view of the human condition,
passionate romance is counterpointed by pain and suffering.

As a sign of masculinity, the knight-at-arms finds himself in a
scene more characteristic of a Romantic poet: isolated in a scene of
nature. That this amounts to a state of alienation rather than simple isolation is suggested by the displacement of the 'pale' to an
adverb describing his activity of 'loitering' rather than it being an
adjective defining the state of his self. The mirroring of the landscape with his subjectivity confirms this. We are asked not just to
consider the state of the landscape, but to think also in terms of the
state of the psyche; and we are asked to consider the displaced
nature of this psyche – its ability to transfer itself onto other people
and things.

At the heart of the poem the knight tells a tale of his meeting
with a lady, but this is already mediated and problematised by the
surrounding frame. We move from an unidentified speaker's use of
the first person – 'I see a lily on thy brow' – to the knight's 'I met
a lady in the meads', and the parallelism between the statements

makes us question the identity of the speaker. Within the embedded story, the object of the knight's attention, the lady, also turns out to be somewhat mobile and uncanny: she's also 'a faery's child' and her eyes are 'wild'. The sequencing of the next four stanzas is also creative of disturbance to our normal expectations of romance. The first ends with 'She looked at me as she did love, / And made sweet moan', which might be considered the nearest we get to a suggestion of consummation, yet it appears at the beginning. And in the next three stanzas an apparent reciprocation between the lovers takes place with the knight setting her upon his steed and the lady finding him 'roots of relish sweet'. When they enter her 'elfin grot' something even stranger takes place in this apparent sharing or alternating of agency. The knight shuts her 'wild wild eyes' with kisses – which we might equate with sleep – after which she lulls him to sleep instead. At one level, there's a slippage here between the two identities: a transference of power and agency. This is developed with the knight's dream in which he sees 'Pale warriors', kings and princes. The knight reports on what he sees and quotes the words of the spectres who confront him; 'La Belle Dame sans Merci / Hath thee in thrall!' Rather than being endorsed by the knight himself, this claim remains only a frightening possibility: that he has been taken in and bewitched by this famed *femme fatale*. As we return to the frame of the poem in which the knight 'sojourn[s] here / Alone and palely loitering', there's the possibility now that he has become a deathly spectre like those in his dream. After this, the opening of the final stanza of the poem with 'And this is why' seems almost perversely playful.

The trajectory of Keats's poem in this respect is in keeping with 'Lamia' and 'The Eve of St Agnes'. In all three poems he takes a mythical or folkloric proposition and opens it out so that it still retains the possibility of its initial meaning, but other, more complicated and more positive interpretations have been made available. Rather than just a tale of encounter with a seductive form of femininity which destroys the heroic figure of masculinity so that he is ultimately wasted or blighted, 'La Belle Dame sans Merci' retains the possibility that the truth or meaning of this encounter lies in romance. The knight's apparent paleness and the sympathetic silence and coldness of the realm of nature which surrounds him all serve to confirm the warmth and vitality of love. From this perspective, the poem illustrates the difficulty of maintaining a realm of romance, besieged as the knight is not only by those he meets, but even by the damning voices of social conformity manifesting themselves in the unconscious of his dreams. Not surprisingly, then, the poem has been read as a commentary on the relationship between the poet and his muse; the poet's inability to maintain his vision in the face of reality; and the poet's glimpse of a realm of truth and beauty only to have to return to a diminished reality.[9]

In this brief and enigmatic ballad Keats manages to include many of the issues of romance and sexual encounter which he was already exploring in the first version of 'The Eve of St Agnes', written two months earlier. In particular, 'La Belle Dame sans Merci' draws attention to the spectral nature of the self and the transformative power of passion – even if negatively conceived here – through its clever manipulation of the ambiguities of perspective.

III. 'THE EVE OF ST AGNES'

When in January 1819 Keats set about an extended attempt at a medieval romance in the form of the poem he always insisted on referring to as 'St Agnes' Eve', he was still concerned about its 'smokeability', its susceptibility to the mockery and scorn of reviewers for its apparent naïvety. As a result, his efforts to push the poem in the opposite direction – towards a more sexually explicit and knowing version of romance – led him into some difficulty before the poem was even published. His publishers Taylor and Hessey strongly objected to the passage where the two young lovers, Porphyro and Madeline, appear to consummate their passion and urged him to revise it in line with polite taste. Keats, perhaps unsurprisingly, responded with obvious anger to what amounted to censorship, before acceding to some of their demands and offering them a revised version of the offending stanzas. Something of his initial fury is evident from the account we have from his friend Woodhouse. Interestingly, his response takes the form of an aggressive and predatory heterosexuality. Not only does he confirm his already determined conviction that he should write only for men, but the measure of the poem and its hero is here defined as crude sexual conquest and a complete absence of ambiguity, almost as if Keats vents his fury at women through a crude deflowering of his own artistry:

> He says he does not want ladies to read his poetry: that he writes for men – & that if in the former poem there was an opening for doubt

what took place, it was his fault for not writing clearly & compre-
hensibly – that he sh^d despise a man who would be such an eunuch in
sentiment as to leave a <Girl> maid, with that Character about her,
in such a situation: & sho^d despise himself to write about it &c &c
&c – and all this sort of Keats-like rhodomontade.   (*Letters*, II, 163)

For all its obvious knee-jerk, heat of the moment aggression, the
passage is nevertheless revealing of the complex ways in which
'sentiment' could be construed in this period. The very idea that
Keats could 'despise a man' for being 'such a eunuch in sentiment'
speaks very powerfully – and even now very recognisably – for the
way in which such a form of heterosexual masculinity polices other
members of the group and urges them to 'prove' their sexuality.
Confirmation of gender identity within the group is here provided
through aggressive hatred and the threat of exclusion seen as emasculation. The oddity for modern readers, on the other hand, is
likely to be the attachment of such aggressive maleness to the
notion of sentiment.[10] The use of this key eighteenth-century term
distances us from what, otherwise, would be a very recognisable
aspect of male heterosexuality. It is easy to read such a passage and
forget that its primary concern is the highly mediated business of
romance poetics. And this, I'm arguing, is perhaps one of the main
problems Keats has to face repeatedly in his exploration of
romance narrative: the remasculinising of sentiment.

One of the most powerful and obvious ways in which 'The Eve
of St Agnes' signals its desire to present sentiment in a more robust,
masculinised manner is in its deployment of a narrative frame for
the story of Porphyro and Madeline. Instead of entering the narra-
tively directly, as in the case of 'Isabella; or the Pot of Basil' where the
first lines are: 'Fair Isabel, poor simple Isabel!', we are presented
with four stanzas focusing on the shivering devotions of 'an ancient
Beadsman'. Keats immediately envelops a tale of warm and
sumptuous passion with a chilling, deathly exterior. No sooner is
'St Agnes' Eve' announced than he establishes the surrounding
atmosphere to the tale with a telling reference to sense perception:
'Ah! bitter chill it was!' The pervasive cold in the realm of nature
represented by the owl and the limping hare continues through to
the old man's prayers, so that his breath 'Like pious incense from a
censer old, / Seemed taking flight for heaven, without a death' ('Eve
of St Agnes', ll. 7–8). Immediately, there's a sly ironising of the religious sentiment in the poem. The old man's cold breath can be read

as a mockery of what should be happening. The poem's imaginative activity, represented most obviously in such similes, seems to contain a playful impiety befitting its title: a strange mixture of the devout and the superstitious turned to erotic account.

As the opening frame progresses, this accentuation of felt coldness at the expense of a more pious focus on the state of one's soul continues with the shift of attention to '[t]he sculptured dead'. This complicates our sense of time and reality. Now we are considering representations of the dead rather than the dead themselves, and we are, most obviously, dealing with another time. In his depiction of them, too, Keats includes the impious possibility that these souls remain trapped, 'Emprisoned in black, purgatorial rails' (l. 15). This freezing spreads to accommodate the more metaphysical possibility that what we are dealing with is a kind of purgatory here on earth, an entrapment which suggests that religion isn't working – either for the beadsman or for the sculptured dead. Primacy is given to sense perception which is most definitely something in touch with the reality of this chill earth. As if to clinch this point, Keats concludes the stanza with a teasingly ambiguous reference to the beadsman's capacity or incapacity to appreciate the feelings of others: 'He passeth by; and his weak spirit fails / To think how they may ache in icy hoods and mails' (ll. 17–18). The line break allows us to cut the meaning at this point or to flow on, thereby offering a creative uncertainty as to whether or not the old man has the power of imaginative sympathy or empathy. The lines also offer a covert commentary on the failure of 'spirit': its capacity for knowledge – thinking – and, in typical Keatsian fashion, the relationship between mere thinking and empathetic projection based on the reality of the senses. In the third stanza, this deliberate confusion about the status of this isolated soul – and of time – takes a further twist with the revelation that, in some way not yet clear, this old man is already dead. At least, his 'deathbell' has been 'rung' and 'The joys of all his life [have been] said and sung' (l. 23). In theological terms, as well as others, the Beadsman seems to be a significantly displaced person, a ghostly, purgatorial presence who resembles the sculptured dead in his haunting of the locus of the narrative.

Even before we encounter the sumptuous domestic and romantic interior of the poem, this frame involving the Beadsman provides its own chilling counterpoint to the tale of youthful passion. The cold, isolated and ageing body of a pious man preparing for death (and seemingly frozen in such preparations) provides an uncanny prelude to an erotic and romantic tale. The ironic and daring playfulness with which the poem handles piety in this opening frame suggests that its purpose is not conventionally moralistic, however. Rather, Keats seems to be posing some uncomfortable questions about the efficacy of conventional religious belief, as well as providing a more literally discomforting sense of bodily experience through which we must pass before encountering youthful passion. He places the wracked and decaying grotesque body in front of us before beginning his romance.

This troubling juxtaposition is perhaps even more clearly evident in the frame which closes the poem. As Porphyro and Madeline 'dissolve' at the end of their narrative, our attention is switched in their stead (in the last four lines of the poem) to the nurse Angela who, we are told, '[d]ied palsy-twitched, with meagre face deform'; and, by way of completing the frame, to the Beadsman who 'after thousand aves told, / For aye unsought for slept among his ashes cold' (ll. 377–8). Here, too, there's a decided twist on the spiritual status of the old man: as if, for all his demonstration of piety, his prayers are left unanswered; he remains 'unsought for', indicative perhaps, of a Godless universe. The reality the poem chooses to deal with (and end with) here is the imaginative certainty of 'cold ashes'. The painful, grotesquely rendered fate of the nurse also supports this metaphysically grim perspective. In the circumstances, her very name – Angela – seems to mock at her limitingly corporeal demise.

This powerful, almost filmic, switch of perspective at the end of the poem is part of Keats's strategic response to the writing of sentiment. Such an abrupt transition from romance into the grotesque (and from erotic imaginative passion to the decaying and diseased body) represents a more strenuous testing out of the nature of sentiment and imaginative sympathy. Keats pushes his audience to the limit by this mixing of emotions attached to the body. It's part of his desire to offer more 'finesse' and a more robust toughening of the audience designed to remove him from the possibility of being 'smoked'. The idiomatic ironising of the tale and its potentially mocking unorthodoxy in its handling of religion, all add to its stock in this respect.

The framed nature of the narrative also provides 'The Eve of St Agnes' with an important level of objectivity and historical self-consciousness. As we have seen, in the first four stanzas of the poem, Keats slips deftly between temporalities while highlighting the intensity of sense perception. This prepares quietly for the denouement in which the lovers 'dissolve' into mere phantoms as soon as they leave the confines of the tale's domestic interior and open the door onto the outside world. The sudden temporal slippage in the doorway provides the poem with a very literal manifestation of liminality for its ending:

> They glide like phantoms, into the wide hall;
> Like phantoms, to the iron porch, they glide;
> [...]
> The key turns, and the door upon its hinges groans.
>
> XLI
> And they are gone – ay, ages long ago
> These lovers fled away into the storm.
> ('The Eve of St Agnes', ll. 361–2, 369, 370–1)

The effect here, produced in conjunction with the frame, is to emphasise the confined space of romance and the degree to which the surrounding environment is not simply uncongenial, but positively threatening. Frequent references to the latent violence of the feudal household and the rift between rival families (reminiscent of *Romeo and Juliet*) are effectively capped with the even greater threat of time and mortality. The emphasis is now firmly on disease and ageing: the very ache of mortality. And the poem's ironic take on religion denies any higher level consolation for its intensely rendered tale of human passion.

The story at the centre of this ironising and toughening frame focuses on a popular superstition: the possibility of maidens viewing their future loved one on 'St Agnes Eve' so long as they carry out the attendant rituals in good faith. The poem's medievalism provides an opportunity to inhabit the hinterland of religion and magic without resting decidedly in either camp. Keats's romance can explore a certain kind of pious devotion coupled with a propensity to see visions which keeps it in touch with the imagination and the fancy without committing itself firmly either to religious conviction or to the supernatural. Indeed, Keats's narrative takes the form of a dominantly anti-metaphysical, secular, particularly physical, even corporeal, rewriting of the narrative as his hero's subterfuge, involving the assistance of the nurse Angela, inveigles him into Madeline's chamber in lieu of what should, according to propriety and folklore, be merely Madeline's fanciful vision of him. In more ways than one, Keats projects a male presence into the sanctum of female fantasy. As we have already seen from his angry response to the potential censorship of his publishers, the condition in which Porphyro (and Keats) 'find' the heroine is one not to be resisted, he argues, by any true man. The superstition attached to the Eve of St Agnes is, ostensibly, a fantasy for young women, but, at one level at least, Keats's poem appropriates this as an aggressive male fantasy of deflowering. Despite this the poem still seeks to retain its capacity to appeal to women readers in its fulfilment of the original folk-legend's female romantic fantasy.

Our first vision of the heroine Madeline focuses precisely and single-mindedly on her state of excited and romantically inclined preparedness. The 'argent revelry' and 'rich array' of the surrounding context are mere 'shadows haunting faerily / The brain, new-stuffed, in youth, with triumphs gay / Of old romance', and, therefore, are ruthlessly dismissed with an abrupt 'These let us wish away, / And turn, sole-thoughted, to one Lady there' (ll. 37, 40–2). As in the case of 'Isabella; or The Pot of Basil', Keats is intent on signalling the fact that he is leaving 'old romance' behind and substituting it with his decidedly modern version. The youthful realm of faery is here rejected in favour of considering the attitude of a young woman whose mind has dwelt all day on love. Already she seems to exist in a strange combination of trance-like immobility punctuated by noises and breathing indicative of sexual arousal or excitement. While her eyes are 'regardless', her lips are 'anxious' and 'her breathing quick and short' and she is already 'sigh[ing]'. In representing her, Keats also provocatively appropriates the language of religion in his worship of beauty and his promotion of erotic romance. Her 'maiden eyes' are described as 'divine'; she longs for her kind of 'bliss'; and young Porphyro arrives in order to worship her. Significantly, the music which she does not hear pervading her chamber is described as 'yearning like a God in pain' (ll. 65–6, 56). The phrase cuts in different directions. It reinforces the way the poem is beginning to deploy the language of religion as the language of eroticism and it suggests that the 'action' of the poem is one which offends against, or is at least removed from, divinity. It also queries the abiding presence of a single, orthodoxly Christian God.

Porphyro's entrance into the poem is very pointedly that: an entrance into the guarded citadel of the castle, into Madeline's chamber, and, fairly obviously by this point, what he deems to be successful sexual consummation with his beloved. In this he is aided, in the stylised manner of such gothic romances, by an old woman who is described as 'weak in body and in soul'. Having been precipitately encouraged to think 'sole-thoughted' about the state of our heroine, Keats now alerts us once again to an attendant spirituality. This romance is repeatedly played out in a context which is haunted by the relics, if not the powerful presences, of Christianity.

In its turn, this is set off against the nature of the inhabitants of the castle. In keeping with the medieval setting and the atmosphere of romance one might legitimately expect chivalry to be among their characteristics. But not so. Keats emphasises the savagery and violence of the inhabitants by associating them repeatedly with an animalistic blood-lust. At the same time as he enters Madeline's 'silken, hushed, and chaste' 'maiden chamber', Porphyro is surrounded by 'barbarian hordes, / Hyena foemen, and hot-blooded lords, / Whose very dogs would execrations howl / Against his lineage' (ll. 85–8). Apart from 'lords', 'lineage' is the only word here one might associate with chivalry and even that is seen in terms of spoliation. Instead of a knightly order, we are introduced to the spectre of a 'blood-thirsty race' in which the one person named – Hildebrand – is 'dwarfish' and suffering from a fever. The threat posed to Porphyro is seen in terms of the grotesque and the monstrous. The realm of romance is interestingly limited here to the besieged young lovers. Even their sole helper Angela is an aged gossip. Keats's medievalism, then, sets up a marked disjunction between piety and the threat of grotesque violence. Whereas 'Isabella; or the Pot of Basil', as we have seen, presents the threat to romance in terms of the exploitative proto-capitalistic social values of the heroine's brothers, here, too, there's a strong suggestion of prevailing male values constituting a code of animalistic violence characterised by cruelty. Keats does not seem interested in exploring this context in his poem; he is content to represent a relatively undifferentiated and unexplained phalanx of male violence as a setting for his love story.

Such is the multilayered context of mortality, disease, potential violence and historical self-consciousness in which Keats chooses to locate his narrative romance. At the heart of the story, Porphyro finds himself secreted in a closet entering onto Madeline's chamber; she, in turn, devotes herself pseudo-religiously to the rituals of

St Agnes' Eve. The 'action' of the poem thus begins from a voyeuristically conceived perspective. From his hiding-place, our young hero watches Madeline disrobe, and we watch, through him, the same visual spectacle. On the part of both hero and heroine there's a peculiar silencing at work. He dare not speak for fear of betraying himself; she offends against the superstition if she utters a syllable. The terms in which Keats represents the conflict within Madeline at this point – Her beating, anxious heart and her stifling of any utterance – are particularly troubling for their mythical, literary associations: 'But to her heart, her heart was voluble, / Paining with eloquence her balmy side; / As though a tongueless nightingale should swell / Her throat in vain, and die, heart-stiflèd, in her dell' (ll. 204–7). The classical story of Philomel who metamorphoses into a nightingale after having been raped by King Tiresias, is disturbingly and somewhat incongruously woven into Madeline's solitary struggle here. There's now an ominous portent of sexual sacrifice, with our heroine as the helpless victim: she's already been described 'like ring-dove frayed and fled' and the nightingale clinches the sadistic excitement here. And although Keats's publishers objected to specific stanzas as breaching the decorum of polite taste because of their sexual explicitness, one of the features of the poem is its presentation of images of sexual excitement and fulfilment throughout its length. Here, the nightingale's little death 'in her dell' adds to the store of images of sexual consummation at the same time as it confirms the strangely hushed action of this section of the poem.

The poem's erotic energy is now dominated and to some extent displaced onto visual spectacle. Keats expends a whole stanza on the 'carven imag'ries' of the casement which serve once again to reinforce the distancing historical perspective at the same time as maintaining the level of sexual excitement – as in the last line, which reads: 'A shielded scutcheon blushed with blood of queens and kings' (l. 216). What follows amounts to a strangely paradoxical beatification of fair Madeline. Though described as 'so pure a thing, so free from mortal taint', she's bathed in the light of the 'wintry moon' which signals mortality. The shift from saint to angel ironically serves only to confirm her status as an object of desire: 'She seemed a splendid angel, newly dressed, / Save wings, for Heaven'. That 'seems' is as indicative as her lack of wings and the phrase 'newly dressed' seems almost comic in its reminder of her womanliness. If any confirmation were needed of the erotic exploitation of the language of religion here, it is provided by the interruptive reminder of Porphyro's reaction: his growing 'faint' (l. 224).

At this point in the proceedings, her prayers said, Madeline undresses tantalisingly in the gaze of her unseen lover and in full focus of the poem's masculine narrative point of view. The teasing element of her stripping consists of its slow deliberateness: she 'unclasps her warmed jewels one by one' and her 'rich attire rustles to her knees' not in one quick movement, but 'by degrees'. In both cases, we are made tellingly aware of the proximity of her jewels and her clothes to her body. The image of her 'Half-hidden, like a mermaid in sea-weed' (l. 231), confirms the mode as one of voyeuristic titillation.

Porphyro having recovered from his faint, Keats now shifts the focus to the psychological state of the heroine who realises the magic of St Agnes Eve by 'see[ing], / In fancy' the person of her lover. She now seems to inhabit a paradoxical state of being to which Keats attaches the word 'perplexed' – as he will later do at a key moment in 'Lamia'. Here Madeline 'dreams awake' and falls into a 'wakeful swoon' (l. 236). At one level, this conflicted and paradoxical state characterises the creative heart of the poem: the point at which dreams come true, reality and fantasy, body and soul, merge together. This conflict is itself a sign of sexual pleasure, of course, which registers itself as a perplexing mixture of otherwise separate emotions: most particularly, pain and pleasure.

At this key point in the poem Keats also depicts Madeline in a state of unconsciousness. Instead of her anxious, troubled, wakeful consciousness, she is described as 'Blissfully havened both from joy and pain; / Clasped like a missal where swart Paynims pray; / Blinded alike from sunshine and from rain, / As though a rose should shut, and be a bud again' (ll. 240–3). Although the image of the rose suggests a libertine fantasy of repetitive deflowering, it is strangely disconnected. Immediately prior to Porphyro's attempts to make her dream a reality, Madeline is strangely removed from the realm of sexuality (pleasure and pain) and becomes an uncanny figure of woman. Not only is she worshipped with a vehemence which is almost pagan in its intensity, she possesses an impossible purity which challenges our very notions of origins and purity. Woman as fabricated, worshipped object of an impossible virtue, is presented to us here. Keats, as we shall see, presents the more obviously uncanny figure of Lamia in a similar way at the opening of

his next major narrative romance. There, Lamia becomes a woman
in a way which destabilises our very conception of woman as a
fixed or even stable gender identity.

With Madeline redefined in this way, Porphyro seizes his opportunity, but proceeds not immediately to her bed for sexual gratifi-
cation, but to lay a table with an impressive spread of exotic
Mediterranean delicacies in two stanzas which have always registered with generations of readers as one of the most memorable
and typically Keatsian set-pieces in the poem. His 'heap / Of can-
died apple, quince, and plum, and gourd, / With jellies soother than
the creamy curd' (ll. 264–6) might well seem incongruous to a
modern reader, especially since, perhaps unsurprisingly, the two
young lovers pay no attention to the food once it is displayed.
There's a strangely displaced eroticism at work here, one which
transposes appetite and a feast of the senses. In his revised draft of
the poem Keats had added a stanza in order to make the ritual,
including the offering of food as sacrifice, more explicable:

> 'Twas said her future lord would there appear
> Offering as sacrifice – all in the dream –
> Delicious food even to her lips brought near:
> Viands and wine and fruit and sugar'd cream,
> To touch her palate with the fine extreme
> Of relish: then soft music heard; and then
> More pleasures followed in a dizzy stream
> Palpable almost; then to wake again
> Warm in the virgin morn, no weeping Magdalen.
> (*Poems*, pp. 622–3)

When, after this delay, Porphyro does make it to Madeline's bed,
his attempts to wake her from her unnaturally deep slumber by
taking 'her hollow lute' and playing upon it might be said to constitute their own form of sexual consummation. At least, her reaction of 'utter[ing] a soft moan' and 'pant[ing] quick' seems to
suggest as much. This moment of implied post-coital recognition
also takes a typically Keatsian trajectory of loss and disappointment, a mortal sadness intruding itself immediately the act has been
completed. In this instance, Porphyro is defined according to his
name by appearing, in the eyes of his beloved, as 'pale as smooth-
sculptured stone' (ll. 294–5, 297) or porphyry. He, too, becomes
objectified, a cold death-object to match the sculptured dead in
the surrounding frame of the poem. Just as Madeline sleeping

represents the disconcerting, impossible figure of woman, so, too, Porphyro hovers between life and death at the same time as his lover sees him in a state of excited confusion between dream and reality. For her, the actual Porphyro appears more like a spectre than the one she has seen in her dream; and the difference is registered in terms which recall the condition of the knight-at-arms in 'La Belle Dame sans Merci': 'How changed thou art! How pallid, chill, and drear!' (l. 311). Madeline's consequent distress at the seeming imminent deathliness of her lover and her calling for him to speak to assure her of his presence, is the spur to the climax of the poem, the stanza which troubled Keats's publishers on the grounds of polite taste:

> Beyond a mortal man impassioned far
> At these voluptuous accents, he arose,
> Ethereal, flushed, and like a throbbing star
> Seen mid the sapphire heaven's deep repose;
> Into her dream he melted, as the rose
> Blendeth its odour with the violet –
> Solution sweet. Meantime the frost-wind blows
> Like Love's alarum pattering the sharp sleet
> Against the window-panes; St Agnes' moon hath set.
>   ('The Eve of St Agnes', ll. 316–24)

At one level this is romantic union of the highest metaphysical kind. It is also a fitting end to a poem based on the power of fancy supported by superstitious faith. 'Melt[ing]' 'into her dream' constitutes the perfect meeting of the fantasy of romance and the reality of the body. In terms of a Keatsian aesthetic, it also represents another form of positively disposed loss of identity, extinction of personality, or negative capability. And although the stanza begins with the idea of Porphyro being 'Beyond a mortal man', the words 'impassioned' and 'voluptuous' drive the passage so that even the line 'Ethereal flushed, and like a throbbing star' is kept powerfully in touch with a very human and erotic sense of the body. As we have seen, the language of Regency bawdy used as a shorthand to describe the delights of sexuality is often characterised by what might seem to us a strangely euphemistic and metaphysical discourse.[11]

It is very typical of Keats's poetry generally that the moment of consummation signalled here by the phrase 'Solution sweet' is no sooner achieved than it is met by the cold wind of mortality. The threat to romance from the outside world is registered immediately as the lovers proceed to make their escape from the most uncongenial of domestic settings. As they do so, they are frozen into the surrounding frame which we examined earlier in the chapter. The sensuous excitement of the poem is immediately undercut not only by the chill wind, but by a historical detachment which is the tough-minded counter-point to their sensuously realised excess of pleasure.

IV. 'LAMIA'

In terms of 'smokeability' and its vulnerability to criticism of its mawkishness, Keats clearly thought that with 'Lamia' he had moved successfully on to a more objective mode. For this extended narrative in two parts he deploys a flexible heroic couplet reminiscent of Dryden, instead of the Spenserian stanza used in 'Isabella' and 'The Eve of St Agnes'. In itself, this change in the formal medium of the narrative might be seen as indicative of a shift in terms of romance as well as the objectivity with which the subject is handled. The move from Spenserian form, and the tendencies of fast-moving couplets, towards a pert, ironising self-consciousness in the narrative perspective, distance the poem even further from 'old Romance'.

The new romance of 'Lamia' might be said to proceed on a number of fronts simultaneously. The danger of Keats's characteristic capacity for empathetic imaginative projection leading him to an immersion in sympathy for his characters is lessened as a result of a more distanced, at times almost Byronic, mode of surface playfulness. The use of a classical setting rather than a medieval one also confirms the poem's daring push towards a more explicit examination of sexuality. Classical licentiousness replaces gothic romance with its prevailing, if failing, Christian ethics. Instead of ironising and playfully displacing conventional piety as he does in 'The Eve of St Agnes', here Keats revels in a classical realm liberated from such conventional moral constraints. The classical here justifies and gives precedence to a more daring form of hedonism. And somewhat ironically, choosing a tale in a more remote classical antiquity allows Keats to be contemporary. Setting his story in ancient Corinth permits him to analyse modern Corinthian values: a culture of licentious masculinity more assured of its worldly experience.

Keats's search for greater objectivity in romance narrative in 'Lamia', instead of leading him away from sympathy, encourages him to engage with it in even more provocative ways. As we shall see, a major part of the drama of this poem derives from Keats's highlighting of sympathy and its problematic relationship with truth. This very deliberate questioning and sensationalising of sympathy is evident in his reworking of a tale he found in Burton's *Anatomy of Melancholy* and which he helpfully appended to the 1820 edition of the poem:

> 'Philostratus, in his fourth book *de Vita Apollonii*, hath a memorable instance of this kind, which I may not omit, of one Menippus Lycius, a young man twenty-five years of age, that going betwixt Cenchreas and Corinth, met such a phantasm in the habit of a fair gentlewoman, which taking him by the hand, carried him home to her house, in the suburbs of Corinth, and told him she was a Phoenician by birth, and if he would tarry with her, he should hear her sing and play, and drink such wine as never any drunk, and no man should molest him; but she, being fair and lovely, would live and die with him, that was fair and lovely to behold. The young man, a philosopher, otherwise staid and discreet, able to moderate his passions, though not this of love, tarried with her a while to his great content, and at last married her, to whose wedding amongst other guests, came Apollonius; who, by some probable conjectures, found her out to be a serpent, a lamia; and that all of her furniture was, like Tantalus' gold, described by Homer, no substance but mere illusions. When she saw herself descried, she wept, and desired Apollonius to be silent, but he would not be moved, and thereupon she, plate, house, and all that was in it, vanished in an instant: many thousands took notice of this fact, for it was done in the midst of Greece.' (*Poems*, pp. 665–6)

There is little room for ambiguity in this version of the tale Keats inherits from his seventeenth-century source. It is simply a question of a lamia or man-devouring serpent in the deceptive shape of a woman successfully preying on her victim. And although there is a glimmering of sensibility ascribed to the lamia in her emotional distress in this earlier account, Keats's main addition to the story consists in his much more sympathetic rendering of the she-monster. This is powerfully reinforced by his inclusion of the death of Lycius in the finale which serves to question even further any simplistic distinction between illusion and reality. It also maintains the poem's ambivalent response to Lamia's presence and power.

Compared to the account he would have seen offered by Lempriere in his *Dictionary*, as well as this version by Burton, Keats's Lamia is a distinctly positive one. The abiding negative characteristic maintained in the poem is her illusory, deceptive appearance; otherwise she is cleared of the more spectacular and grotesque attributes of the figure, such as its tendency to devour men or even children.

Keats's complications in his handling of the story are immediately signalled. In giving the poem her name, Keats declares his interest in the nature of his Lamia. It is as if she ceases to be merely a generic label for a figure of monstrosity. That possibility remains to haunt the narrative, but Keats's creativity and, in particular, his imaginative sympathy, particularise Lamia's selfhood to the extent of individualising it. Imaginative sympathy and sentiment in this poem are to be stretched across some disparate and uncomfortable territories. The mixture of the grotesque and the romantic in the final framing of 'The Eve of St Agnes' makes for a strangely ambitious uncomfortableness which seems to have been part of Keats's design: a difficult transition from romantic sentiment to disgust. Here, the very identity of the poem's main character contains and accommodates that kind of disturbing mixture. Reading over his manuscript of the poem in September 1819, Keats was up-beat about its ability to generate a reaction in its readers: '... I am certain there is that sort of fire in it which must take hold of people in some way – give them either pleasant or unpleasant sensation. What they want is a sensation of some sort' (*Letters*, II, 189). The sensationalism of the poem he produced might be said to offer the pleasant and the unpleasant in equal measure and at the same time, particularly as regards its central female figure. Lamia is a study in impossible identity. Rather than a single self, the figure of Lamia throughout works upon an uncanny set of possibilities combining woman and monstrous serpent.

This question of identity and its related problem of sympathy are drawn to our attention near the beginning of the poem where in an extraordinary set-piece metamorphosis Keats describes Lamia becoming a woman. This is typical of the poem and the way in which it handles subjectivity. The excitement here is generated by the process of becoming, by the pyrotechnics of Keats's verse seeing the self as change. Keats's rendering of this extraordinarily pleasurable and painful metamorphosis is equally struck between the exotic differences of surface textures and the supposed internally felt nature of identity conveyed through feeling. It is both internal and external in a way which seriously challenges our conception of the relationship between those two things as they relate to the self. This spectacular metamorphosis near the beginning of the poem provides a good indication of how the poem's narrative is intent on questioning subjectivity in relation to interiority and origins:

> Left to herself, the serpent now began
> To change; her elfin blood in madness ran,
> Her mouth foamed, and the grass, therewith besprent,
> Withered at dew so sweet and virulent;
> Her eyes in torture fixed, and anguish drear,
> Hot, glazed, and wide, with lid-lashes all sear,
> Flashed phosphor and sharp sparks, without one cooling tear.
> The colours all inflamed throughout her train,
> She writhed about convulsed with scarlet pain:
> A deep volcanian yellow took the place
> Of all her milder moonèd body's grace;
> And, as the lava ravishes the mead,
> Spoilt all her silver mail, and golden brede;
> Made gloom of all her frecklings, streaks and bars,
> Eclipsed her crescents, and licked up her stars.
> So that, in moments few, she was undressed
> Of all her sapphires, greens, and amethyst,
> And rubious-argent; of all these bereft,
> Nothing but pain and ugliness were left.
>
> ('Lamia', I, ll. 146–64)

The terms of this transformation are a very particular paradoxical mixture of pain and pleasure which asks to be read as indicative of sex. In this respect, Lamia's foaming mouth produces a fluid both 'sweet and virulent' and she 'writhes about convulsed with scarlet pain', where the adjective serves to clinch the transformation of apparent pain into a signal of sexual pleasure. This, in turn, is reinforced with 'ravishes', 'licked up' and 'undressed'. At one level, we're being asked to read this as a moment of sexual excitement which sets the terms for identity and 'truth' for the rest of the poem. If we are expecting this metamorphosis to establish a clear revelatory definition of the status of our lamia then we are likely to be disappointed. Instead of confirming her origins, this passage occludes them; and it does so by reversing some of our standard conceptions about identity while confirming others to do with gender and a masculine perspective on the uncanny figure of woman defined through her body.

The alarmingly negative conclusion to the glorious excitement of Lamia's transformation defines her new condition of womanhood as one of painful loss. To be a woman is to leave her beauty behind: to become subject to loss. The metamorphosis is, it turns out, a kind of stripping in which the essence of this creature remains strangely undefined. There's a disturbing inversion at work here: in a story of a man-eating predatory lamia one might legitimately expect the narrative to begin with the putting on of a disguise of false beauty with which to lure and deceive the hapless male prey. Instead, Keats has his creature lose its dazzling beauty so as to become a woman. When, at the end of this early section of the poem, Lamia speaks for the first time, it is a moment of eerie self-presence. What might otherwise have been read as a reassuring sign of identity now becomes an uncannily disembodied voice:

> Still shone her crown; that vanished, also she
> Melted and disappeared as suddenly;
> And in the air, her new voice luting soft,
> Cried, 'Lycius! Gentle Lycius!' –
> ('Lamia', I, ll. 165–8)

From a wider perspective, Keats's representation of Lamia might be read as symptomatic of how his culture sees the figure of woman. In this instance, the tale enables him to explore not only the deceptive, alluring figure of the *femme fatale* who is capable of undermining masculine identity, but also the very nature of femininity. Lamia's metamorphosis focuses on the degree to which woman is all surface and no substance.

Our first acquaintance with Lamia presents her as consisting of a bewildering variety of textures. She is so many things at once in terms of beauty that she becomes self-cancelling:

> She was a Gordian shape of dazzling hue,
> Vermilion-spotted, golden, green, and blue;
> Striped like a zebra, freckled like a pard,
> Eyed like a peacock, and all crimson barred;
> And full of silver moons, that, as she breathed,
> Dissolved, or brighter shone, or interwreathed
> Their lustres with the gloomier tapestries –
> So rainbow-sided, touched with miseries,

She seemed, at once, some penanced lady elf,
Some demon's mistress, or the demon's self.
('Lamia', I, ll. 47–56)

Beauty, dazzling as it is, is a thing of mere surfaces and guarantees
no interiority, no essential identity or 'character', and no soul. The
poem also makes some disturbing assumptions about the nature of
pleasure, particularly about its 'perplexed' nature. As I've already
suggested, this might be seen as a coded signal for reading such
ambivalent sense perception as sexual excitement or pleasure. In
the case of Lamia, however, such interinvolved combinations of
pleasure and pain seem to be the very condition of her existence.
Other than the surface of dazzling, even self-cancelling, varieties of
beauty, there is nothing. To that extent she resembles the uncanny
doll/woman Olimpia in Hoffmann's famous tale *The Sandman*
which encapsulates the sense of constructed femininity as a conspiracy aimed at narcissistic male desire. In that instance, the unfor-
tunate Nathaniel gazes on the doll and reads her seeming assent
and passivity as the longed-for other half of his romantic passion.
Even her automaton exclamations of 'O, O, O' are understood,
according to his fantasy, as the signs of pleasure. In the case of
Lamia, her *raison d'être* might be said to be, then, the very process
of pain/pleasure. To this extent, she might be considered as a more
specialised and focused representation of woman as the epitome of
sexual pleasure and knowledge: woman made in the light of the
male gaze; 'not as she is, but as she fits his dream'.

The Corinthian setting of the poem confirms this sense of specialised sexual pleasure and its associated knowledges. In the
ancient world, Corinth was synonymous with the erotic and was a
well-known centre of prostitution. In Keats's day, too, 'Corinthian'
maintained these connotations and was a by-word for a man of
worldly pleasures: a young buck about town. This has led some
critics, most notably Marjorie Levinson, to read 'Lamia' contextu-
ally and sociologically as a poem of prostitution and the commodification of passion.[12] From this perspective, Lamia's downfall is
determined by her quest for respectability within marriage. Society's
guilty open secret is exposed in the doomed and inevitable climax
to the tale.

As if to confirm the poem's specialist concern with sexuality, Keats
provides it with a mini-narrative involving Hermes and a nymph
before Lamia's main narrative gets underway. This establishes – and

to some extent justifies – a dynamic of aggressive roving male desire. The 'ever-smitten Hermes' burns with passion and grants Lamia her wish to return to 'woman's form' in exchange for her help in locating the invisible nymph. The consummation of this pursuit encapsulates the disturbing combination of sentiment and aggression, pain and pleasure which characterises the poem as a whole. Faced with an impassioned Hermes, the young nymph 'Faded before him, cowered, nor could restrain / Her fearful sobs, self-folding like a flower / That faints into itself' (I, ll. 137–9). The emphasis here on fear rather than ambivalent pain is indicative of a worrying level of sexual domination which is also to feature in the main narrative of the poem. At one point, Lycius treats Lamia with an equivalent level of sexually charged cruelty. His passion is described as 'cruel grown', '[f]ierce and sanguineous' as he delights in Lamia's sorrow in a passage reminiscent of the second stanza of 'Ode on Melancholy'.

This opening narrative establishes, then, the sexual mores of the whole poem as one of uncontainable and aggressive male desire in the realm of the gods which is construed more generally as sexual pleasure – even, one presumes, for the fearful, pursued nymphs. Just as important is this section of the poem's presentation of the previous existence and motivation of Lamia herself. The bargain she strikes with Hermes is, on both sides, about the need to satisfy desire, but, in her case, it is dignified with the name of love, albeit love associated with 'bliss' or sexual fulfilment: 'I love a youth of Corinth – O the bliss!' (I, l. 119). This positive motivation of her love for Lycius is something the poem does very little to challenge; it is much more interested in the false nature of her identity, the sham nature of her woman's form. What her status as a lover does give her, however, is the power of romance removed from origins and social context. The terms on which Lamia bargains with Hermes, however, also include the following important revelation: 'I was a woman, let me have once more / A woman's shape, and charming as before' (I, ll. 117–18). Although Lamia is presented as a blushing, 'swift-lisping' serpent with a 'Circean head' immediately prior to this speech, the possibility of her being a woman before she was a serpent remains as another kind of haunting possibility throughout the poem, especially if we go so far as to believe that her request for the god to give her 'my woman's form' is to return her to her original state. Whether Lamia has both a serpent's and a woman's form remains unresolved. What she is as a fixed identity is, in this way, removed from her capacity to love.

As a lover, Lamia turns out to be much more than a beautiful female form in love. As the Corinthian setting would suggest, this is a story of the arts of love and the heroine of this new kind of romance is appropriately well versed in erotic culture. Somewhat typically, of course, she also conforms to the required idea of the modest virgin. Soon after her spectacular transformation, the narrator's attention turns to consider the pleasure in store for his young hero: 'Ah, happy Lycius.' The perspective is clearly defined as one which sees Lamia's function as one of producing pleasure in her male lover. After an initial detailing of her pastoral innocence, the poem moves on to a much more specialised territory of sexual knowledge and expertise:

> ... – for she was a maid
> More beautiful than ever twisted braid,
> Or sighed, or blushed, or on a spring-flowered lea
> Spread a green kirtle to the minstrelsy:
> A virgin purest lipped, yet in the lore
> Of love deep learnèd to the red heart's core;
> Not one hour old, yet of sciential brain
> To unperplex bliss from its neighbour pain,
> Define their pettish limits, and estrange
> Their points of contact, and swift counterchange;
> Intrigue with the specious chaos, and dispart
> Its most ambiguous atoms with sure art;
> As though in Cupid's college she had spent
> Sweet days a lovely graduate, still unshent,
> And kept his rosy terms in idle languishment.
>   ('Lamia', I, ll. 185–99)

Even before this poem's famous denouement in which different kinds of knowledge are pitted against each other in the form of the sage Apollonius and the two lovers, here Keats offers an almost scientific commentary on the physiological nature of sexual pleasure. Admittedly, there's a wry humour at work in the passage which thrills to the impossibility of this phantasm of innocence and purity performing bodily pleasure as if she is familiar with the very nature of matter. Keats seems to be enjoying this fanciful and rare coming together of the corporeal and the intellectual, not least for its display of knowledgeable worldliness. There's a controlled display of sexual knowledge here which is very unlikely to be criticised as mawkish.

This is also true of a passage a little later in this first part of the poem where Lamia does her best to convince Lycius that she is a woman. Throughout this passage her argument is augmented by singing, whispering, and 'other speech than looks' to create, as ever, an uncanny sense of her somehow being just a woman and more than a woman. Just such a combination creates intense 'delight' for Lycius and Keats uses the moment – somewhat ironically it has to be said – to advertise his poem's sexual knowingness and its difference from the fantastical representations of femininity to be found in the literature of romance:

> Then from amaze into delight he fell
> To hear her whisper woman's lore so well;
> And every word she spake enticed him on
> To unperplexed delight and pleasure known.
> Let the mad poets say whate'er they please
> Of the sweets of Faeries, Peris, Goddesses,
> There is not such a treat among them all,
> Haunter of cavern, lake, and waterfall,
> As a real woman ...
>
>   ('Lamia', I, ll. 324–32)

One of the abiding paradoxes of Keats's love poetry and, in particular, his exploration of verse romance, is the detour and indirection through which we have to travel to be presented with 'a real woman'. In this instance, there's an amusing irony at work in Keats's conjuring of the 'real' in a context where the whole force of the narrative is dominated by the insecurity of the 'woman's form' inhabited by Lamia. The mixed nature of Lamia's identity enables Keats, as in this instance, to move between a worldly eroticism and the fantastical. Keats's form of romance is committed to an exploration of these competing, sometimes contradictory, elements of woman's complex and conflicted identity as it appears to the male imagination. His poem operates precisely in the realm of uncertainty created by the unresolved combination of woman and lamia.

In the much-debated and somewhat inevitable conclusion to the story, Keats furthers this uncertainty. His tale of Lamia and Lycius does not depend upon narrative suspense as regards its closure. Theirs is a doomed relationship and, in case the reader hasn't reached that understanding early on, Keats is quite explicit about the outcome in the opening commentary of Part II. All of which compounds the doom-laden sense of the ending to the extent that Keats is able to concentrate on other ways of questioning the truth of what happens. The most famous of these consists of an interruption to the wedding feast by drawing attention to the plants which should adorn the temples of his protagonists: willow and adder's tongue for Lamia; the thyrsus removed from Lycius so as to allow him to forget; and, most tellingly, spear-grass and 'spiteful thistle' for the sage Apollonious. It's as if the poet intervenes decisively on the side of the lovers and against the cruel rationality of the sage by making this pre-emptive strike at the meaning of their actions:

> Do not all charms fly
> At the mere touch of cold philosophy?
> There was an awful rainbow once in heaven:
> We know her woof, her texture; she is given
> In the dull catalogue of common things,
> Philosophy will clip an Angel's wings,
> Conquer all mysteries by rule and line,
> Empty the haunted air, and gnomèd mine –
> Unweave a rainbow, as it erewhile made
> The tender-personed Lamia melt into a shade.
>   ('Lamia', II, ll. 229–38)

The initial question here is already loaded in a typically Keatsian way with its conjuring of the romantically associated word 'charms' and with its playful inclusion of sense perception as the test of truth. What appears to be an attack on philosophical reason for its spiritless demystification of wonder in the case of the rainbow is also focused on its reduction of the erotically charged 'tender-personed' Lamia into a mere shade. Such a reduction of Lamia to an insubstantial nothing, as we have seen, was actually one of the poem's starting-points. Equally, Lycius's sexual pleasure (as well as that of the worldly-wise narrator) has focused on the recognition of the pleasure that a 'real woman' is capable of producing in a man, as opposed to the mere faeries, peris and goddesses of literary romance. To this extent, then, the apparent attack on Apollonius and his disbelieving, anti-romantic rationality is something which the poem has already deployed in its wider function of articulating the paradoxes and contradictions which surround the uncanny figure of woman in the narrative of Lamia.

As the narrative reaches its climax, Keats also complicates the conflict between reason and experience (represented by Apollonius) and romance (represented by both lovers) by the way he represents the sage philosopher. This is focused particularly on the gaze of the participants. The downfall of the lovers might be said to depend upon Lycius's insistence on marriage: the bringing of their passion into the public gaze rather than allowing it to continue untroubled in the private realm of romance. What follows is an exercise in the power and truth-bearing capacity of looking. When Apollonious stares fixedly into Lamia's eyes (traditionally held to be the windows of the soul), he is met with an inhuman gaze, the lidless eyes of the serpent. The irony of Keats's handling of this confrontation is that he presents both Apollonius and Lamia as soulless, inhuman gazers. There's a further level of disturbing correspondence between accuser and accused here; a fact seized upon immediately by Lycius as he warns his fellow Corinthians of the demonic nature of his tutor: 'look upon that grey-beard wretch! / Mark how, possessed, his lashless eyelids stretch / Around his demon eyes!' (II, ll. 287–9). Although we have to contend with the obvious possibility that it is Lycius who is possessed or bewitched by Lamia rather than the philosopher, the poem goes on to offer some confirmation of his observation by confirming that 'his eyes still / Relented not, nor moved'. More pertinently, the final act of the poem, Apollonius's ascription of the category serpent to Lamia (which can be viewed from the perspective that he is a good reader of allegory) at which she shrieks and vanishes, is offered, most disturbingly, in the language of sexuality conceived in terms of male mastery and female pain: 'the sophist's eye, / Like a sharp spear, went through her utterly, / Keen, cruel, perceant, stinging' (II, ll. 299–301).

In this context, the death of Lycius might be read as much as a support to the poem's belief in the nature of love between its two young protagonists as confirmation of the Lamia's power to undo the masculine self. Keats's complex transfer of her demonic qualities to the figure of the philosopher at the poem's close confirms his sense of the difficulty of romance within prevailing social conditions. Although a philosopher and representative of reason, Apollonius seems to speak on behalf of the presiding male authority of the culture. In that capacity, he represents a slightly different threat to romance than that conceived in 'Isabella' and 'The Eve of St Agnes' where, as we have seen, the young lovers are faced with the power of money and the barbaric violence of feuding families respectively. In many ways, this opposition in 'Lamia' is a more difficult form of conflict: a battle between two forms or kinds of intellectual activity, two modes of truth. Reason and imagination are here brought together to stare each other out.

The outcome of this, as one might expect of a poem which has gone so far to culture uncertainty, is far from clear-cut. Lamia's withering and disappearance might be thought of as confirming the ultimate fact of her existence, her being a snake rather than a woman. But Apollonius's 'triumph' might only provide further evidence of the sadly destructive power of a narrowly defined version of reason. The 'sharp spear' of the philosopher might be held responsible for two deaths at the end of the poem. The power of romance might be less than this: more fragile and more precarious, but no less valuable. Lycius's death might even be seen as indicative of the power of love. That the finale of the poem should consist of Keats providing the eye of reason with the discourse of aggressive male sexuality in an act of painful penetration is a testament to the degree to which he is willing to subject poetic romance itself to the test of a new kind of sexual realism.

4

Endearing Addresses:
the Odes

The form of the ode is particularly suited to the exercise of an empathetic and projective imagination, and Keats's odes have not surprisingly become synonymous with what is taken to be his most characteristic mode of creativity. This irregularly structured lyric, which takes the form of an address, provided Keats with an opportunity to explore the relationship between the self and other. In this respect, the excited fluctuations and identifications between the speaker and addressee in the 'Ode to a Nightingale' have been seen as instancing the workings of the Romantic imagination – that creative power which allows the poetic self to transcend its limitations by becoming that which it contemplates. This chapter focuses on the significant, but often underplayed, presence of gendered subjectivity in the odes which forms part of Keats's continued engagement with the power of love as it manifests itself here in the form of sexual encounters, wild ecstasy, young lovers, happiness and appetitive desire. The chapter will also look at Keats's self-proclaimed deployment of a feminised fancy rather than on imagination. This accords with the leniency and precariousness in the workings of the odes, their tentative, though excited, exploration of relationships and their rigorous scrutiny of their speculative knowledge. In keeping with the way they work in alliance with the fancy, the odes are acutely aware of the deceptions, the feigning, at the heart of the knowledge they debate. And in terms of the self and the figure of the poet which feature prominently in these poems, the emphasis of the analysis below will, similarly, be on the proximity of identity rather than its definite or confident presence. Just as we

have seen passion, relationship and objectivity combined successfully in his narrative romances so, in Keats's odes, the presence
of the poet is often interestingly removed from the object of
attention – at times, even occluded.

I. 'ODE TO PSYCHE'

Keats's 'Ode to Psyche' begins the sequence of the great odes: 'Ode
on a Grecian Urn', 'Ode to a Nightingale', 'Ode on Melancholy'
and 'To Autumn'. Originally entitled simply 'To Psyche', it seems
to have begun life as a sonnet and to have developed into the more
extended and irregular form of an ode. Often overlooked and considered to be of less significance and achievement than the other
famous four, it plays a key role in establishing not only the form,
but the central issues and vocation of these extraordinary poems. It
is a dedication to a new kind of love poetry in which Keats explores
the idea of worshipping Psyche, a late pagan goddess who missed
out on the worship of poets and prophets. '[T]he Goddess was
never worshipped or sacrificed to with any of the ancient fervour –
and perhaps never thought of in the old religion – I am more ortho-
dox that to let a hethen Goddess be so neglected', he explained in
a letter to his brother George and his wife Georgiana (*Letters*, II,
106). The speaker of the poem sees himself as remedying this loss
by acting as her 'priest' and by building a shrine in which to worship her. Keats's interest in Psyche is thus caught up in the idea of
her belatedness, her displacement from an earlier time of true piety
and belief. In choosing Psyche as the object of his poetic devotions,
then, Keats attaches himself to a particular sense of historical displacement. It is not simply a question of moving in seemingly
escapist fashion from his own contemporary situation to the poetic
realm of ancient Greece. In the object of his worship, Keats finds a
form of historical lack with which to match and explore his own.
The late classical period of lapsed beliefs and forms of worship
matches that of early nineteenth-century London.

This is very deliberately brought to our attention by the way the
poem exploits its temporality. The address to the goddess is immediately followed by a reference to 'to-day', and the second stanza's
apostrophe, 'O latest born and loveliest vision far / Of all Olympus'
faded hierarchy!', deliberately merges Psyche's late classical era
with the present. This is then clinched in the third stanza with a

reminder of the figure of the poet: 'Yet even in these days so far retired / From happy pieties, thy lucent fans, / Fluttering among the faint Olympians, / I see, and sing, by my own eyes inspired' (ll. 40–3).

In choosing Psyche as his idol, Keats is also very pointedly addressing the belief-system of his own age and culture. This is a provocative exercise in paganism: not a decorative use of classical pastoral, but a concerted attempt to explore the nature of the soul free from Christian orthodoxy. In his letters, Keats had reacted against the standard Christian view of the originally unique identity of the soul and the idea of this life as a vale of tears which is passed through on the way to better things. Religion's compensatory offer of consolation in afterlife was repugnant to him, even if the notion of an afterlife itself was not. Keats's brief articulation of a more unorthodox humanism by contrast sees this life as a 'vale of soul-making' in which suffering stamps identity upon the soul to constitute a major part of life's achievement. Identity in this scheme of things is not something simply assumed or already acquired, but something to be achieved, even constructed. Keats thought it 'a grander system of salvation than the chrystain religion', one that 'does not affront our reason and humanity'. Central to his scheme is the role played by suffering in this process of 'Spirit-creation'. The soul, for Keats, is a place where the 'heart must feel and suffer in a thousand diverse ways!' (*Letters*, II, 102). The ode's dedication to Psyche, then, the Greek word for soul, confirms this metaphysical interest and establishes its grounds of experience in relation to beauty, truth, and love. It is a daring act of poetic dedication flying in the face of religious orthodoxies and conventional morality.

The poem's other daringness – and one that jars most modern sensibilities – lies in its insistence on seeing things with the eye of fancy. The poem relies on conjuring (in almost voyeuristic fashion) a distinctly casual, chance sighting of the gods embracing in what appears to be a post-coital slumber in a forest. As ever, Keats is careful to query the category of fancy as he does through the odes: 'Surely I dreamt to-day, or did I see / The wingèd Psyche with awakened eyes?' (ll. 5–6). Later, he returns to a more confirmed sense of the visual with 'I see, and sing, by my own eyes inspired', and although the tendency of the poem is to stress the act of internalisation, the building of a temple or 'fane' within the mind, the poem's central scene is one of casual vision imposing itself on the

senses. The poem's ending once again draws attention to the artifice, the seeming, of 'the gardener Fancy' whose power is to 'feign'.
It also provides a reminder of the limits of this mental reality. 'Soft
delight' is soon significantly qualified by 'shadowy thought'. This
highly sensuous creative realm possesses only the insubstantiality
of the workings of a mind. The poem's conjuring of the fancy, as
much as its pagan classicism, has led critics to undervalue its initiation of the project of the odes, and, in particular, the way in which
that project is couched in the language of romance.

Just as Keats's imaging of himself as a priest of Psyche might be
thought of as a kind of retreat from the contemporary, so, too, it
might be seen as confirming his vocation as poet as opposed to his
life as a lover. Typically, the configuration in Keats's texts is more
complex than that. As we have already noted, the central scenario
of this ode consists of two lovers – Cupid and Psyche – locked in
each others' arms (and wings). Even more provocatively, the ending
of the poem also contains the possibility of disturbing the relationship between priest and goddess, poet and muse. The fluidity of the
relationship between subject and object here allows – as it does in
many of the odes – for interpretations which see Psyche about to
receive 'Love' in the form of Cupid, or a scene in which the poet
seeking inspiration and a restoration of his fanciful vision awaits
his lover/goddess at the opened casement. Keats's dedication to his
poetic vocation takes the form of an amatory assignation, his worship of the deity an act of eroticised wooing. The promise of
'A bright torch, and a casement ope at night, / To let the warm
Love in!' (ll. 66–7) carries with it something more romantically
generalised, familiar and available than a specialist act of devotion
to a classical goddess. Throughout, the poem operates on this paradox of the language of eroticised romance. What appears to be a
renunciation of romantic love and sexuality – Keats imagining himself in the role of dedicated priest and a member of a specialised,
unpopular sect – takes the form of a reinscription of erotic romance. The terms of this new religion of romance are far from an
ascetic denial of sexual pleasure. Instead of leaving such things
behind, the poem reignites them as the language of poetic inspiration. To that extent it makes creative capital out of the apparently
conflicted energies of the lover and the poet.

The situation of the poet in this ode is thus interestingly poised
on the edge of romance. If the main impetus and poetic structure
of the poem are built up through a series of apostrophising

addresses to the goddess which confirm the poet's calling, the inclusion of a scene of passion between Psyche and Cupid or Eros positions the speaker/poet as an onlooker, curious, excited, but removed from the entwined experience of the lovers. Excited proximity rather than detachment is the order of the day here. Keats's figure of priest, poet and prophet vicariously enjoys a state of rapture and excited intimacy. The creative act of the poet consists of building a shrine to match the leafy bower of bliss in the first stanza. His 'branched thoughts' and the 'wreathed trellis of [his] working brain' (l. 60) conjure an expectant scene of sexual encounter which falls between subject and object, poet and goddess, worshipper and the worshipped.

Here it is important to take account of the original context of the odes. Significantly grouped alongside them in the 1820 volume *Lamia, Isabella, the Eve of St Agnes, and Other Poems* are a number of poems which appear to be of a less rigorous and exacting nature. Criticism has tended to remove the odes from this context and to clear the canonical poems from the possible taint of these more relaxed, casual, and fanciful pieces. The most significant of these for our purposes are the two sonnets on fame and the rondeau entitled 'Fancy'. This last poem in particular provides an interesting insight into the workings of the 'Ode to Psyche', different though it undoubtedly is in terms of form, tone, and ambition. The force of fancy to Keats can easily be undervalued. The trajectory of most Romantic criticism has been heavily inflected by the Coleridgean promotion of Imagination above the merely mechanical Fancy, a critical move which has also had lasting consequences for understanding the aesthetics of much eighteenth-century poetry. The very lightness and looseness of this poem which leads Keats to describe it as a rondeau confirms its status within the category of the fancy, but not derogatively so. Keats clearly cherishes such attributes as liberating and creative.

The modified couplet which frames the poem – 'Ever let the Fancy roam, / Pleasure never is at home' – is a testament and incitement to Keats's belief in the liberating power of fancy which he then catalogues in the first part. Fancy's power is to make present what is absent, to make seen that which is unseen. Within the paucity of night or winter it can instantaneously present the 'April lark' or 'Freckled nest-eggs' (ll. 44, 59). Such ability to transcend the limitations of the seasons is nothing slight. In a letter to his friend Benjamin Bailey in March 1818 Keats had written, at a moment of self-doubt, of the peculiar power of looking:

> I am sometimes so very sceptical as to think Poetry itself a mere Jack a lanthern to amuse whoever may chance to be struck with its brilliance – As Tradesmen say every thing is worth what it will fetch, so probably every mental pursuit takes its reality and worth from the ardour of the pursuer – being in itself a nothing – Ethereal thing may at least be thus real, divided under three heads – Things real – things semireal – and no things – Things real – such as existences of Sun Moon & Stars and passages of Shakspeare – Things semireal such as Love, the Clouds &c which require a greeting of the Spirit to make them wholly exist – and Nothings which are made Great and dignified by an ardent pursuit – Which by the by stamps the burgundy mark on the bottles of our Minds, insomuch as they are able to 'consec[r]ate whate'er they look upon'. (*Letters*, I, 242–3)

The 'Ode to Psyche' clearly exhibits the poetic possibilities of this moment of doubt. Its ardent addressing of the goddess and its testament to the power of the mind explore the intense but delicate reality that poetry is capable of. It is very much Keats's consecration of the soul in love through the visualising power of the fancy.

In the second part, fancy's power is more specially and problematically focused on feminine beauty. That fancy is here herself feminine is significant. The power of mobilising or releasing fancy up until this point in the poem is figured as a male prerogative, a form of masculine authority. Now Keats turns his attention to feminine beauty and its mortality, in particular its being subject to decay or its tendency to pall with familiarity: 'Where's the cheek that doth not fade', 'Where's the face / One would meet in every place?' (ll. 69, 73–4). The poem locates the possibility of an ideal of feminine beauty beyond real women and their bodies. In their place is the possibility of 'a mistress to thy mind' which only fancy can deliver. The culmination of the poem takes the disturbing form of releasing fancy, now expressly realised as a feminine form in such a way as to disturb and place in doubt the difference between fancy and the kind of mistress she will deliver to the male gaze. The disrobing of Hebe 'when her zone / Slipped its golden clasp, and down / Fell her kirtle to her feet' disturbingly parallels the instruction to 'Break the mesh / Of the fancy's silken leash; / Quickly break her prison-string' (ll. 85–91).

In this poem, 'Fancy' clearly champions the idealised nature of beauty, but it does so in a way which understands the appetite for beauty as a familiar form of roving male desire, a subspecies of libertinism which laments satiety and the palling of excitement and which must never rest content with a single lover or wife. The aesthetics of fancy mirror the economy of desire to be found in libertinism. The injunction of the poem's framing couplet might be read as a young man's insistence on liberation from marriage and the domestic hearth as the site of romance. Keats's insistence on romance is emphatically differentiated from a poetry of the affections which it would clearly see as limitingly domesticated. The figure of fancy here as well as taking the form of a woman is also a captive bird which must, like the figure of the male poet, be released from the limitations of 'home'.

To read this poem alongside the odes, and the 'Ode to Psyche' in particular, is helpful and revealing. Most obviously, it offers support to the ode's celebration of the power of fancy, the liberating force of its capacity to realise in visual terms that which is not present. It also provides specialist support for the visual nature of pleasure in this poem, the idea of a shocked, intense looking at a scene of two lovers on the brink of sexual communion which lies at the heart of the poem. Having read 'Fancy', it is also easier to see how this feminine realm of the fancy is combined with a displaced form of roving male desire. The aesthetic at one level, it seems, is offered up as a remedy for the inevitable disappointments of romantic love and sexual passion. Keats's realm of fancy at once challenges conventional male identity in its deployment of a feminine and feminising aesthetic and confirms it in its reinscription of an economy of desire forever fending off the death of satiety by its search for new objects. Keats's conjuring of the multiple and paradoxical nature of beauty here can, from this perspective at least, be seen as a corrective or solution to the unhappy narrative of male heterosexual desire.

The configuration of lovers in 'Ode to Psyche' is also significant for our understanding of the later odes. Here the relationship between the poet/speaker and the object of his address is predicated on a visual encounter. Although the poem opens with a more expected Keatsian emphasis on the aural – 'O Goddess! hear' – the culmination of the opening stanza is to be found in the revelation of her identity as the second, female lover in the embrace: 'but who wast thou, O happy, happy dove? / His Psyche true!' (ll. 22–3). The rationale for the poem, then, is provided by this prior, visual encounter. We might also speculate about the speaker's relationship in this encounter with Cupid and Psyche. Here it is, of course, the poet who remains 'unseen' and not the object of his attention, unlike the nightingale. His familiarity with Cupid might also require some explication. Is Keats here making a point about Cupid being no longer the mischievous boy, but the lover Eros now that he has found his true love in Psyche? In itself, this might lead to an assumption of more likely identification between speaker and pagan deity, but the dynamic of the poem lies most definitely between him and Psyche. This makes the stumbled-on scene in the 'deepest grass' even more interesting. Even if the true object of the poet's song has not been caught in *flagrante delicto*, more in post-coital slumber, the scenario here is at least partly disturbed by a sense of erotic triangulation. Leaving aside the possibility that the scene's visual emphasis pushes it dangerously towards voyeurism, the arrival of the third party certainly leads to a complex substitution. The speaker recognises the male lover, then the female lover as the true love of the former, while dedicating himself to her.

II. 'ODE ON A GRECIAN URN'

The kind of certainty with which Keats addresses the goddess 'Psyche' is completely lacking from the 'Ode on a Grecian Urn'. Here, creative uncertainty prevails. For most critics and commentators, this is the most enigmatic and perplexing of the spring odes.[1] Much of the reason for this lies in Keats's choice of subject – the urn – and the complicated way he addresses it and shifts his focus of attention upon it. At various points in the poem, we are asked to consider the urn as an object, the frieze around its outside (including the images of a sacrifice, an empty village, maidens and lovers), and, ultimately, the possibility of its containing the ashes of the dead. This last facet is reserved till the end and is, even then, only implied. And this is typical of the workings of this ode: the poem revolves around its deathly centre considering the different attitudes of its subject. It is more interested in the periphery, the frieze or border, and those attendant upon it than the thing itself: more interested in those coming to the sacrifice than the event itself. In this respect it is much more decentred than 'Psyche'. The thing addressed here is multiple and shifting, not a fixed identity: more an object which mediates other possibilities, such as the lovers depicted on its side. To this extent, it is a much more complex poem of address. Less fixed in the security of its object, the poem is liberated to construct itself through its terms of address and endearment. The ode's basis in apostrophising now takes centre-stage as the creative force of the poem. Although the 'Ode to Psyche' is marked by excitement and surprise, 'Ode on a Grecian Urn' provides a much more hectic and various manipulation of shifts in tone. In that aspect alone, this is the most irregular of the spring odes and the one most remote from the restrained, implied knowingness of the later 'To Autumn'.

Most importantly, perhaps, Keats's attention is seized from the start with the problem of knowing or understanding the cultural significance of this survivor from a remote past. As with his sonnet 'On Seeing the Elgin Marbles' where his response is registered as a 'dizzy pain', Keats seems to revel in a kind of intellectual overload resulting in a stymieing of reason. From a purely rationalist perspective, this is exacerbated by Keats's delight in the bafflement of the historical imagination which such archaeological objects produce. This problem of understanding is already well developed in the poem before it reaches its famously puzzling conclusion. Critical debate has often centred on the status of the poem's ending where the aphoristic, eminently quotable 'Beauty is truth, truth beauty', is followed by the dangerously enticing 'that is all Ye know on earth, and all ye need to know.' The critic's dilemma has also been increased by the existence of different versions of the poem's ending with differently situated quotation marks.[2] As a result, the problems of knowledge which the ode generates at its heart are complicated by these further sets of questions about who speaks and who says what. Are the quoted words an inscription on the urn or an implied meaning extrapolated from the story told by this 'sylvan historian'? Does the rest of the ode support this statement or undercut it? The fact that the first stanza ends in an excited series of questions suggests that the poem's mode is interrogative rather than authoritatively aphoristic, though the quoted words might be thought by many to be sufficiently enigmatic and inscrutable in themselves.

Keats's exploration of romance and sexuality is continued from the outset of 'Ode on a Grecian Urn', with the first lines of the poem taking the form of an address to 'Thou still unravish'd bride of quietness'. Critics have often pointed out how the ambiguity of 'still' here (once again promoted through a creative lack of punctuation by the omission of a comma after 'still'), meaning 'as yet' (as well as, in eighteenth-century usage, 'unmoving', 'continually', and 'always'), mobilises the gap between past and present. Whereas, in the 'Ode to Psyche', Keats combines beauty and a remote deity, here the very terms of this opening apostrophe join the promise of sexual encounter with the abstraction of 'quietness'. The transposition of a sexual and romantic topos was already significant in the earlier poem, though still embodied in a single identifiable feminine form. Now, the same ambivalently poised liminality pertains, but the extent of distancing and mediation is much greater. To be a bride of quietness pushes the realisation of imaginable romance to the limit, as does the revelation in the next line that 'she' is not simply the child, but the 'foster-child' of silence and 'slow time'. Keats delights in complicating the relationship so that it becomes unfixed, less susceptible to directness and certainty.

At the opening of the ode, then, the problem or even the very impossibility of sexual encounter is signalled with the combination of 'unravished bride'. The status of the object addressed remains problematically mediated and subordinate instead of a figure or identity in its own right. Keats has swapped a confident recognition of the goddess for something which is, in more ways than one, an object: something defined in relation to a subject rather than having a confirmed identity of its own. Identity would here be confirmed by having something done to it: according to the poem, the act of being – or not being – ravished. On a more literal, archaeological level, it's a question of the urn or vase remaining intact from the ravishings or ravages of history. At the same time, Keats has removed the speaking male subject of the poem even further from the entanglements of romance. In 'Psyche', the speaker voyeuristically encountered the slumbering goddess entwined with her lover Cupid. Here, too, the speaker commentates at a distance from the urn's depictions of 'maidens loth', lovers 'overwrought' and in 'mad pursuit'. He focuses in particular on a pair of lovers the condition of whose sexual happiness is always on the brink, but never at the point of consummation. They remain 'Forever panting', forever about to kiss. This pushes the scenario of Cupid and Psyche whose 'lips touch'd not, but had not bade adieu' to a more pointed, urgent enquiry about the limits and thresholds of sexual activity and the way in which such acts alter our identity and place us in different categories: chaste/unchaste; ravished/unravished; innocent/experienced.

Once again, Keats transposes and substitutes questions of history and sexuality so that they can interrogate each other. In the case of the 'Ode to Psyche', as we have seen, Keats was attracted to the late classical period because it provided him with a justification for dedicating himself to a goddess somewhat neglected because of the lapsed state of religion. It also enabled him to make a pointed comparison between that late period of antiquity and his own situation in early nineteenth-century England, especially when his poem is concerned to explore his own rather unorthodox ideas of the soul. Here, in 'Ode on a Grecian Urn', Keats focuses on the earlier period of classical religion in order to point up the gap of historical difference which pertains. The identities of the participants, their geographical location, and the meaning of their ceremony resist knowledge. And exactly what it is which empties this village of its inhabitants on this 'pious morn' remains unknowable. The religious impulse of the scene engendered by the urn is thus figured as arcane and resistant to interpretation although, as one might expect from Keats, its Dionysian qualities are apparent from the start and form the crescendo to stanza one which ends significantly with the phrase 'wild ecstasy'. From the outset, then, Keats figures the occult religion of ancient Greece as one characterised by sexual encounter and pleasure.

This is developed in the second stanza's focus on the aural. In 'Psyche' the visual predominated and the power of fancy consisted in making present to the sight what was not present. Here, in more pointed paradoxical fashion, Keats focuses on the 'unheard' in a way which provides a bridge between the imagined music of pipes and the situation of a male lover engaged in 'song'. As ever, Keats projects from a distance onto the figure of the male lover, situating himself outside of the realm of romance. The vantage-point of history seemingly gives the figure of the poet the authority to pronounce upon the very nature of romance. In contrast, the figure of the lover is presented as if trapped within his historical moment. He cannot be separated from the thing he is performing. Our speaker, in marked contrast, stands as if released from song into a higher historical knowledge. To this extent, Keats is also, of course, offering a commentary on the role of the poet in parallel to that of the lover. Lover and poet are both seen from the two perspectives: to sing is to lose one's separate identity in song; to love is to lose one's separate identity in romance. From his privileged historical vantage-point the speaker proceeds in stanza three to ruminate upon the nature of happiness thus curtailed. In 'Psyche' Keats had applied the epithet of 'happy, happy' to the goddess herself. Here he devotes a whole stanza to the idea.

In keeping with the way in which the ode feeds off paradox, this idea of the 'happy, happy' uses repetition to signal a question. There's clearly a troubling excess in this doubling of happiness. To be happy is fine; to be happy, happy is deeply problematic, the repetition suggesting a kind of cancelling rather than an increase in rapture. The excited exclamations of the stanza's fifth line: 'More happy love! more happy, happy love!' multiply the implied questioning of the status of this unchanging state of happiness which, on the face of it, has so far been wistfully presented as overcoming the usual transitoriness and changeability of human passion. Now the nature of this passion is defined in relation to time and is characterised by the suggestion of a frozen moment: 'for ever' awaiting fulfilment – 'still to be enjoyed.' Although the poem seems to privilege this strangely unchanging passion by describing it as 'far above' human passion, the climax to the stanza returns us emphatically to the physical condition of the human rendered as one of sorrow and the physical, mental and corporeal effects of the expenditure of passion's energy. Though ostensibly negative in its representation of the experience of human passion, the poem's querying of the implicitly inhuman passion that remains fixed forever in the excited moment of anticipation leads to an anxiously poised weighing of the two kinds of experience. That brink between excited anticipation and disappointment is one that Keats would soon explore in his 'Ode on Melancholy'.

Through its compacted language of paradox, excess and implication, 'Ode on a Grecian Urn' performs in a surprisingly brief circuit an extraordinarily rich examination of the relative merits of passion conceived of as the agitated, changeable, and ultimately failing human kind and as the idealised, immobile representation of art. Passion as lived experience and passion as aesthetic object are subject, as we have seen, to a rigorous scrutiny which includes a high level of historical self-consciousness. In this respect, perhaps, the ultimate play of the poem and its delight in decentring itself as a system of address lies in its openness to being subsumed by that idea. The significant inclusion of the preposition 'on' in its title means that from one perspective the whole poem can be read as a historicised inscription: no more (or less) than the writing on the side of the classical urn. The poem thus has the potential to finally open itself out as an enigmatic *objet d'art* surrounding its hollow centre, known to be the receptacle for the ashes of the dead. In this respect, the subject of the poem performs the ultimate act of identification with his object of address. Although addressed to an inanimate object, this ode provides Keats with an opportunity to examine with real force art's capacity and incapacity to deal with the messy business of human passion.

III. 'ODE TO A NIGHTINGALE'

Keats's 'Ode to a Nightingale' might be thought of as the ode which most obviously and fluently manifests the form's potential for moving between the polarities of subject and object. Keats's choice of a nightingale confirms his interest in the realm of nature, but this is, inevitably, nature mediated through art. The bird heard singing in his friend's garden in Hampstead might have inspired the poem even to the extent of its being originally titled 'Ode to *the* Nightingale', but, as the poem points out, it is a bird whose presence in history has been marked by its literariness, from classical myth and into English poetry through Milton and Coleridge. The identification between poet and bird is, then, already well established before the poem begins. In terms of the difference between the two, Keats seems to have originally begun the poem with the idea of a dryad, a nymph associated with trees and, according to his source Lemprière, one capable of marrying. Although the main axis of the poem rests on the relationship between poet and bird, the human and the natural, the transient and the immortal, this possible gendering of the nightingale forms an interesting undercurrent in the poem, one which surfaces in provocative ways in the final stanza where it is associated or even identified with – depending on how one reads the syntax – the feminine power of the fancy:

> Forlorn! The very word is like a bell
> To toll me back from thee to my sole self!
> Adieu! the fancy cannot cheat so well
> As she is famed to do, deceiving elf.
> ('Ode to a Nightingale', ll. 71–4)

Critical opinion has, on the whole, baulked at Keats's use of the rhyme word 'elf' here. In what stands, for many, as a prime example of a poem about the workings of imagination, it introduces a disconcerting realm of faery. But, as in 'The Ode to Psyche', Keats is here expressly dealing with the workings of 'fancy'. The presence of an alluring or, at least mischievous, 'elf' reinforces the larger idea within the poem of the nightingale's alluring song being something which represents a dangerously attractive form of enchantment which tempts the speaker to follow the nymph deeper into the forest towards death or oblivion. The idea of the nightingale as a beguiling feminine form which 'feigns' reality in the manner of the fancy is certainly worth considering, even if it isn't quite manifested in the form of woman as in the 'La Belle Dame sans Merci' and other *femme fatale* poems. Though most often read as a prime example of imaginative identification, 'Ode to a Nightingale' repeatedly articulates itself in terms of the pull of attraction which would lead the speaker to join, not become, his 'light-wingèd Dryad'. The idea of 'fade[ing] away into the forest dim' in stanza two is expressed as 'with thee', not 'as thee'. This is reinforced by the split between the nightingale and its song which is the focus of stanza seven. The transhistorical presence of the nightingale focuses on the 'self-same song' heard '[i]n ancient days' by 'emperor and clown' and 'Through the sad heart of Ruth'.

This problem with the nightingale and its song is registered in the opening stanza where Keats continues his interrogation of happiness. As in the 'Ode on a Grecian Urn', this problem takes the form of a worrying excess: ''Tis not through envy of thy happy lot, / But being too happy in thine happiness'. Keats once more exploits the doubling of 'happy'. There's also a creative uncertainty as to who is the subject of this second line: is it the bird or the poet (or both) who is too happy in appreciating the nightingale's happy lot? In the case of the former, the problem would take the form of a self-absorbed, solipsistic, even narcissistic, complacency; in the case of the latter, it would signal an almost pathological extremity in the poet's capacity for sympathetic imagination or empathy. In this respect, the condition of the poet is equally worth attending to. It is, perhaps, possible to miss the force of the idea of heartache despite the fact that these words form the first phrase of the poem. More attention has been paid to the paradoxical state of numbness associated with creativity and with the rich poetic melancholy which emerges from the use of painkillers and sedatives. It is easy for all this to mask the dichotomy between the poet's heartache and the nightingale's happiness. More importantly, the poet's condition at the beginning of the poem is defined by a potentially contradictory state of heartache and numbness, that is to say, pain or sorrow and its absence: sensibility and insensibility. This in some ways prefigures the paradoxical creativity of melancholy and indolence which forms the territory of the two later odes. Here also the poet makes a poem out of an apparently negative state poised ambivalently on the borders of consciousness.

By the third stanza the problem with the poet has migrated to Keats's persistent concern in the odes with the burden of historical self-consciousness. Whereas the Grecian urn could also be considered as a historian telling a tale, the nightingale exists only within history and can't stand outside it as a presiding intelligence. Its ignorance is a kind of bliss where bliss is really a troubling happy happiness. The bird's ignorance, then, is also immediately conceived of as a limitation, particularly in a context where Keats's idea of soul-making is founded on the notion of constructing identity through suffering.[3] The self-conscious knowledge of being human is now brought to bear on the subject, making the heartache of the first line more a condition of our existence than a particular response to romantic love. A rather despairing account of suffering mortality follows:

> Here, where men sit and hear each other groan;
> Where palsy shakes a few, sad, last grey hairs,
> Where youth grows pale, and spectre-thin, and dies;
> (ll. 24–6)

At this point, Keats introduces a clinching statement on the nature of the human condition, the curse or fallen condition of our humanity, in a line which reads like a prescient precursor of modernist angst: 'Where but to think is to be full of sorrow.' In such words, it can be seen how the Grecian urn's enigmatic power to 'tease us out of thought' – to perplex to the extent that we are relieved of the burden of thought – can be thought of as a blessed relief. The end of the stanza removes us from these more general existential questions in order to return us to Keats's preoccupation with feminine beauty and romance seen from a determinedly masculine perspective. '... Beauty cannot keep her lustrous eyes, / Or new Love pine at them beyond to-morrow.'

IV. 'ODE ON MELANCHOLY'

In his next two odes – 'Ode on Melancholy' and 'Ode on Indolence' – Keats deals more overtly and concertedly with the

subject of romance and its conflict with his ambitions and identity
as a poet. In this sense, these two poems represent a valuable
contribution to this important aspect of his achievement in the
odes. For most critics, however, these last two of the spring
sequence represent a perceptible falling off in quality, with
'Indolence' most definitely at the bottom of the pile. While there
are many different aesthetic issues contained in this evaluation,
there is nevertheless a connection between their standing and their
connection with romance. One of the most harshly judged aspects
of 'Melancholy', for example, is the climax of its third stanza
where Keats includes the idea of a male lover 'emprison[ing]' the
hand of his female partner. Gittings has referred to this as 'painting
a rather silly and "Cockney" picture of the young poet flirtatiously
holding on to his girl-friend's wrists while she struggles to get
away'. One can empathise with Gittings's sense of a disturbing
male force here,[4] and the presence of this obtrusive aggression is at
odds with the way in which critical opinion has valued the odes for
their ability to transcend the details of their time. There's a suggestion that 'Melancholy' is being downgraded because it remains too
caught up in the embarrassing particularity of early nineteenth-
century sexual conduct.

There is, though, more to the poem than this. The 'Ode on
Melancholy' continues Keats's exploration of the marginal or limi-
nal state of mind characterising creativity which, in the previous
ode to the nightingale, is marked by a peculiar combination of
sensitivity and insensitivity he chooses to describe in the corporeal
terms of aching and numbness. The context of an external evening
pastoral setting which features in 'Ode to Psyche' (and which might
be said to form the presiding backdrop to 'Ode to a Nightingale')
is one of speculative creative musing which has a long and distin-
guished history within eighteenth-century poetry, including Gray's
'Elegy Written in a Country Churchyard', Collins's 'Ode to
Evening' and Barbauld's 'A Summer Evening's Meditation'. Such
poems create the rich possibilities of a well-developed literary representation of melancholy which Keats is able to draw on. Precisely
because of these literary precedents, he is able to expose the
doubleness – the paradoxical and deeply ambivalent nature – of
this supposedly negative state of mind. He does so in a more condensed and contracted form to the other odes and one which pares
down the expansive movement between polarities to be found in
the nightingale poem. Here the subject of the poet/speaker remains

implied. The obvious I/Thou axis of the earlier poem has been replaced with the implied subject of the speaker engaged in an oblique relationship with his ostensible subject of melancholy. Instead, the poem takes the form of an address, sometimes cautionary, sometimes admonitory, offering advice to a male figure defined most particularly in the second and third stanzas as a lover. As in other poems, Keats removes himself from the situation of the lover in order to explore the subject of romantic love at a discreet distance.

The poem opens and proceeds, then, through a series of complex negatives which make present the catalogue of the props of melancholy. As the centre of the first stanza makes clear, this is an inverted version of the ending of his first spring ode; he envisages a 'mournful' instead of a happy Psyche to which the poet/lover dedicates himself. The speaker presents himself as a knowing, experienced initiate offering advice to the novice. The peculiarly specialist paradox of this kind of aesthetically productive melancholy consists in heightened perception rather than oblivion, as the last line of the stanza suggests. The 'wakeful anguish of the soul' is to be cherished rather than escaped. The burden of self-consciousness articulated in 'Ode on a Grecian Urn' – 'Where but to think is to be full of sorrow' – is here seen from its reverse, more positive, angle. There's clearly a sense of relishing while suffering this paradoxical anguish of self-consciousness. The movement of the poem is towards more intense experience; the idea is to find ways of experiencing this melancholy at its most rarefied and extreme – something the poem clinches in terms of bodily appetite in the word 'glut'.

For most of the first two stanzas we are provided with little context for the object of the speaker's advice, though the general territory is one suited to a devotee of an aesthetic of melancholy whom we might legitimately assume to be at least analogous to the poet. Only with the arrival of the word 'mistress' in line 8 of the second stanza does Keats choose to offer more definition of his supposed auditor. The application of the advice about melancholy to a context of romantic love, which follows, serves to place such love within a similarly aestheticised, self-conscious discourse of role-playing. Our modern sensibilities, like Gittings's mid-twentieth-century response, might be to object to this rather ungallant, laddish expression of superior physical force coupled with a refusal to take his female partner seriously. Romantic love is being treated as a game in which negative emotion is the luxurious delight of the significantly removed male onlooker:

> Or if thy mistress some rich anger shows,
> Emprison her soft hand, and let her rave,
> And feed deep, deep upon her peerless eyes.
>
> (ll. 18–20)

The power relations are certainly disturbing, as is the suggestion of a sadistic, non-mutual pleasure at the woman's expense. This dramatic shift in the poem continues with the final stanza taking for its subject the mistress as the embodiment of love.

In this third and final stanza the subjection of the female lover and her implied demonisation in the phrase 'peerless eyes' (with her unnatural gaze carrying the suggestion that she could be some demonic gorgonesque figure of woman) is reinforced by the speaker's seemingly confident assertion that this nameless 'She' is to be associated with death and decay. Within the specific context of a poem dwelling on the search for a more specialised form of melancholy, this is positive rather than negative, of course. However, a sense of a *femme fatale* conspiracy – or spell – is never far away from the poem's final revelation of the proximity of melancholy and delight. It is (in line with earlier parts of the poem) seen as an occult knowledge. Typically, this is imaged in gustatory, epicurean form as the male lover breaking 'Joy's grape against his palate fine'. The final twist consists in the shift in power relations of this act of connoisseurship. The ultimate experience of melancholy the poem has to offer presents the male lover as victim, or at least subject to – in thrall to, according to 'La Belle Dame sans Merci' – his chosen female idol. And, to this extent, the poem reverses the situation at the end of the second stanza where feminine identity was the subject of male appetite.

One of the odd things about 'Ode on Melancholy', especially given the rich poetic provenance of melancholy and creativity, is its resolute maintaining of a distance from its subject of the male lover and seeker of melancholy. For all the implied knowingness of its initiated speaker, it refuses to mobilise the figure of the poet and make his anxious quest for fame and achievement an integral part of its narrative of the workings of melancholy. Wordsworth had done precisely that in the opening stanzas of 'Resolution and Independence' where he equates not just dejection, but madness with the business of being a poet. There, too, he articulates an earlier version of Keats's insight into the proximity of joy and melancholy in his lines: 'As high as we have mounted in delight / In our dejection do we sink as low' ('Resolution and Independence', ll. 24–5), where the proximity and mental precariousness of the poet's mind are neatly encapsulated in the space it takes to move between one line and another. The fragility of a line break is the distance between joy and despair in Wordsworth's version. In Keats, by contrast, melancholy remains almost detached from human agency.

V. 'ODE ON INDOLENCE'

In what seems to have been the last ode written in the spring of 1819, 'Ode on Indolence', Keats shifts the ground considerably. This is seemingly the most biographical of the odes and certainly marks a studied return to the use of an ode centred on a first person, 'I' persona. And in terms of the exploration of the conditions of poetic creativity and identity in these odes, most particularly the state of mind of the poet, this is the most explicit and most indicative of a crisis. It is somewhat surprising, then, that it is the ode which has attracted least critical acclaim.[5]

This most likely has something to do with the idea of 'indolence'. As we have seen, melancholy is pushed by Keats to a specialist extreme; he makes it a part of his strenuous search for sensation. The very opening of that ode makes clear the precision and intensity which are to be fostered in this paradoxically creative negative state of being. Keats situates melancholy on the brink of consciousness with all the paraphernalia of excess and he cleverly combines it with all the emotive and ambivalent energy of romance and sexual encounter. Although it could be argued that indolence also has a rich heritage in earlier eighteenth-century verse (Thomson's 'The Castle of Indolence' being its most obvious precursor), the nature of Keats's indolence precisely lacks the energised and sexually related excess of his version of melancholy. By contrast, critical opinion has tended to prize the tensed, paradoxical movement between polarities: hence the high reputation of 'Ode on a Grecian Urn' and 'Ode to a Nightingale'. In those poems the movement between mortality and artifice, intense, passionate existence and death or oblivion, constitutes the success of the ode. Here, in his 'Ode on Indolence', Keats deals with a state of mind which is immediately less appealing to the intellectually rigorous and, perhaps, even more simply, less recognisable. There's a strangeness here which is well worth examining.

In his letter to George and Georgiana Keats of 19 March 1819 Keats provides a detailed description of this state of his temper which forms the basis of the ode he was to enjoy writing two months later:

> This morning I am in a sort of temper indolent and supremely careless: I long after a stanza or two of Thompson's Castle of indolence – My passions are all alseep from my having slumbered till nearly eleven and weakened the animal fibre all over me to a delightful sensation about three degrees on this side of faintness – if I had teeth of pearl and the breath of lillies I should call it langour – but as I am *
> I must call it Laziness – In this state of effeminacy the fibres of the brain are relaxed in common with the rest of the body, and to such a happy degree that pleasure has no show of enticement and [...] pain no unbearable frown. Neither Poetry, nor Ambition, nor Love have any alertness of countenance as they pass by me: they seem rather like three figures on a greek vase – a Man and two women – whom no one but myself could distinguish in their disguisement. This is the only happiness; and is a rare instance of advantage in the body overpowering the Mind. (*Letters*, II, 78–9)

There's certainly a physiological precision here. Keats's medical training informs his detailed description of a state of being which pushes beyond his interest in numbness in the earlier odes. He defines a state of mental and physical deprivation as a kind of liberation: something rare in the literary canon before the arrival of Samuel Beckett's would-be catatonic anti-heroes. In keeping with his problematic attitude towards thought which features strongly in the 'Ode on a Grecian Urn' where the ancient art object 'dost tease us out of thought', this passage ends with an explicit celebration of the body's dominion over the mind. Liberation takes the form of pure bodily consciousness, a kind of unknowing, in which, as he puts it at the beginning of the passage, to be 'supremely careless' is an achievement. Even at this level of physiological detail, however, Keats operates within a distinctly gendered conception of identity; this state apparently brought on by the pervasive softness of 'animal fibres' is described in the prevailing terminology of his time as 'effeminacy'. (He is even alert to the gendering and rank differentiated sense of the term 'laziness', jokily suggesting that the word 'langour' might be more appropriate for female beauties.) This strange state of relaxation and softness which removes Keats from the pressures of ambition, poetry, and love is described in terms of the 'delightful', clearly part of the feminised aesthetic of the fancy. In terms of an economy of desire, the effeminate is also clearly defined as a zone of passivity and inertia.

The poem, as opposed to this fascinating passage from the letters which precedes it, presents the state of indolence in rather different terms, but Keats's attention to the diminishing pulse is still present, as is his unsettling celebration of a degree zero of being in the last line of this extract from stanza two:

> Ripe was the drowsy hour;
> The blissful cloud of summer-indolence
> Benumbed my eyes; my pulse grew less and less;
> Pain has no sting, and pleasure's wreath no flower:
> O, why did ye not melt, and leave my sense
> Unhaunted quite of all but – nothingness?
>   ('Ode on Indolence', ll. 15–20)

Already the poem is beginning to formulate indolence as an escape or release from the miseries and cares of life. Freedom from pain is soon followed in stanza four by a yearning for 'an age sheltered from annoy' and a delight in not knowing 'how change the moons' and a desire to avoid 'the voice of busy common-sense'. The pleasures and freedoms of indolence are clearly a mixed bunch. To avoid 'the fever and the fret' among the agony and pain of mortality, as articulated in 'Ode to a Nightingale', at least carries with it an anguished urgency which is certainly not quite matched by indolence's 'annoy' and 'busy common-sense'. Here we meet with annoyance and delightfulness, not death and beauty combined. The overall suggestion of the non-urgent and the whimsical is not helped by the penultimate stanza's development of the state of indolence as a crowded pastoral dreaming in which 'My soul had been a lawn besprinkled o'er / With flowers, and stirring shades, and baffled beams'. The disturbing and disorientating corporeal liminality of a state in which the poet is aware only of 'nothingness' has been left far behind.

The main thrust of the poem instead consists of the vision of the figures of Love, Ambition, and Poesy who present themselves, revolvingly, three times in the manner of figures on an ancient Greek vase. The psychic drama of the poem consists in their appearing in the first place, the poet's recognition of their identity, and, finally, his resistance to them as he banishes them from his sight. As such, the poem demonstrates the controlling force of the poet's self over its troubling ghosts. As a poem of crisis, it stages a resolution of the potential conflict in Keats's poetic aspirations and ambitions. It reasserts the autonomy of the self in the face of their temptations. More worryingly, perhaps, it removes itself from these ghosts so as to inhabit a position of achieved indolence which it equates with happiness.

Although the poem articulates the poet's yearning to join the figures in the manner of the nightingale ode – 'to follow them I burned / And ached for wings' – its trajectory moves in the opposite direction towards a renunciation of poetry. She, like Love, is clearly marked out as feminine, whereas (in the poem at least) ambition needs no gender definition and is therefore supposed to be masculine. The comparison between the two female forms is also clearly marked by Keats: 'The first was a fair Maid, and Love her name.' When he comes to 'poesy' the relationship is much more ambivalent and embedded:

> The last, whom I love more, the more of blame
> Is heaped upon her, maiden most unmeek –
> I knew to be my demon Poesy.
>
> (ll. 28–30)

The conflicted nature of the poet's engagement with poetry is mediated as a provoking sexual attraction aroused through 'her' sullied reputation. His 'demon Poesy' is written as disturbing 'minx'. Once again, however, for all the engagement suggested by his description of poesy as his 'demon', the poem frees the male poet far too easily from the attraction of his aesthetic lover. Rather abruptly, the demon is shrugged off with: 'For Poesy! – no, she has not a joy – / At least for me – so sweet as drowsy noons / And evenings steeped in honeyed indolence' (ll. 35–7).

The final stanza dismisses all three figures as mere 'Phantoms' with the reassurance that there are plenty of visions in store aside from them. That all are deceiving, false perceptions of themselves is reinforced by the poet's forceful assertion that he 'would not be dieted with praise, / A pet lamb in a sentimental farce'. (The same phrase had been used by Keats in a letter to Sarah Jeffrey explaining his developing ability to treat the response of his reviewers with a more mature disdain.[6]) False praise emanates from this false version of ambition, the ode suggests. The same is, presumably, true for the other members of the threesome.

Such a turn on the dissembling, false nature of the very things he is drawn towards confirms, of course, one of the important strands present in all the odes: the real danger of self-deception. The 'deceiving elf' of 'Ode to a Nightingale' is also a deceiving self, as the poem's rhyme makes clear. As I have indicated, many of the impulses of the odes, particularly their starting-points, originate in the delicate, feminine and always potentially delusive workings of the fancy. The sequence of spring odes begins with the fanciful embodied in a vision of Cupid and Psyche which it eventually questions by exposing the fancy's capacity to engage in mere 'feigning'. It ends in similar fashion, dismissing a vision of false gods in a way which draws attention to the dangers of self-involved and solipsistic identity. 'Ode on Indolence' is the most hard-hitting and at the same time the most escapist of the odes. As such, it forms a fitting, if unsatisfactory, conclusion to the sequence.

VI. 'TO AUTUMN'

'To Autumn', written in September 1819, has been seen as the poem in which Keats fulfils his exploration of the ode form. Most critics have regarded it as the most accomplished and the one in which Keats most obviously realised his tendency towards a self-projecting and self-abnegating mode of creativity. Here, it is argued, Keats best exemplifies his preference for a non-didactic, non-hectoring kind of poetry whose creative capacity can be best measured by its imaginative ability to appreciate the otherness of things and to speak as it were from the identity of those things through sensuously rendered images rather than through argument. Whereas 'Ode on Indolence' is the most autobiographical, self-referential, and self-willed, 'To Autumn' takes the occlusion of the 'I' of the speaker/poet, explored earlier in 'Ode on Melancholy', to its limit. The hectic questioning, passionate excitement and energetic fluctuations of 'Ode on a Grecian Urn' and 'Ode to a Nightingale' give way to implied complexity. This is the least agitated, if not least anxious, of the odes.

Identity is absorbed most fully into the system of address which the unidentified speaker carries out, with autumn evident in its processes as they make themselves apparent to the human through the senses and, most intriguingly, through the personification which takes place in stanza two. For many critics, this personification provides a troubling and baffling axis for the poem. Keats's complex and condensed rendering of competing representations of autumn from the classics, English poetry, and the visual arts, creates a figure which remains enigmatic in terms of gender identity. Helen Vendler sees autumn as definitely female, a version of the Roman goddess Ceres; John Barnard regards the figure's hovering 'between male and female' as symptomatic of the balanced nature of the poem.[7]

The invitation or injunction to the reader which opens this second stanza – 'Who hath not seen thee oft amid thy store?' – opens out the possibility of vision rather than locating it within the poet, as is the case with those visions of the fancy which, as we have seen, form the basis of the odes on Psyche and indolence. Keats's personification, then, seems to act at the heart of this poem as a point of mediation between the realm of nature and the human. Figuring autumn in this way allows him to offset what would otherwise be too stark and conflicted a contrast between nature and the human in the poem. The personification never quite takes on the definite nature of an allegorical figure; instead, it subsumes various versions of the human labours of the harvest within it. Without this halfway-house between goddess and mortal, there would be no human presence and activity within the ode. Stanzas one and two represent a self-contained nature undergoing its internal or implied processes.

Perhaps the moment of most disturbance within the poem, the first line of stanza three – 'Where are the songs of Spring? Ay, where are they?' – itself only a brief relique of the hectic questioning of earlier odes, presents us with the possibility of another interruptive, possibly disruptive voice, and one which enables the reader to access the poem's muted but most obvious point of self-referentiality. This is the one point where the business of poetry and literary ambition erupts, but even here it is still located within nature. The line echoes Milton's 'Lycidas' and in so doing clinches the poem's literariness and its subtle connection with pastoral elegy. Mortality and death feature prominently, as we have seen, in the spring odes – often as the counterpoint to youthful passion and beauty. Death is, like the speaker of the poem, the implied presence behind the goings-on of the natural world which, of course, in the case of autumn are necessarily poised between fertility and impending death. Working by implication, the end of the poem offers us the prospect of the departure of the swallows and links this through rhyme with the word dies. As with the nightingale's linking of 'high requiem' and 'sod', 'To Autumn' joins the sky with death. This reinforces what has already been quietly suggested in the stanza as the gnats, lambs, crickets, robins and swallows all offer their version of pastoral elegy. '[F]ull-grown lambs' will soon be dead meat.

If 'Ode on Indolence' offers an explicit account of the poet's crisis with love, poetry, and ambition and ends with a wilful dismissal of their false appeal, 'To Autumn' offers its own form of renunciation. Romance and desire are, like the involved poet speaker, absent from this scene. Keats's compound noun 'bosom-friend' is the closest we get to the presence of a human bond, and even this is used to define the relationship between the sun and the season. For all the conspiracy of nature's fecundity and its push towards an unnerving excess – 'For summer has o'er-brimmed their clammy cells' – no lovers, only bees, are taken in by this version of happy happiness. Personified autumn, too, is itself a displaced representation of labour. S/he is to be found 'sitting careless', 'sound asleep', 'Drowsed', looking, watching or, at most, steadying her 'laden head'. The role of autumn as displaced onlooker serves to remove the implied speaker even further from the scene. Work, like ambition and desire, has been disconnected. Even if one reads 'To Autumn' as an implied version of pastoral elegy, nature somehow removed even from the indolent figure of autumn personified reveals no necessary or sympathetic attachment to the human. The potentially elegiac songs of nature are never quite allowed to be fixed into a meaningful relationship with the human anxiety over death and mortality. They remain resolutely the songs of the creatures themselves, performed for their own purposes. The poem's designed passivity, its projection of identity into the things addressed, offers the reader the temptation of turning things implied into meaning, things impending into things arrived. As William Empson once famously suggested, death lies at the heart of the pastoral.[8] In the case of Keats's 'To Autumn' the statement rings true, but the subject is never directly addressed.

5

Corresponding Selves: Keats's *Letters*

> I wish I knew always the humour my friends would be in at opening a letter of mine, to suit it to them nearly as possible. I could always find an egg shell for Melancholy – and as for Merriment a Witty humour will turn any thing to Account – my head is sometimes in such a whirl in considering the million likings and antipathies of our Moments – that I can get into no settled strain in my Letters –
>
> (*Letters*, I, 324)

As this excerpt illustrates, Keats's letters are a complex coming together of writer and readers in which the sense of audience is as acute as the self-conscious production of a body of writing. Keats's keen imagining of the moment of reception is matched by a sense of coherence which is at least psychological, if not literary.[1] The above statement itself, of course, has the peculiar status of a meta-commentary on letter-writing, though embedded in a very particular letter. The pull of letters in contrary directions is also clearly evident here: their being things of the moment; their being thought of as a body of work; and their need to match the mood of the participants. Keats captures the strategic nature of these texts: their willingness to suit in order to bond a relationship and the peculiar kind of creativity which is produced out of their very limit and contingency, the way in which they encourage a humour which can 'turn any thing to Account'. Keats plays with and creatively exploits the physical and temporal contingency of early nineteenth-century letters: their cost and the limits of space; the time they would take to arrive and the moment of delivery. Two of his most loved correspondents, his brother George and his sister-in-law

Georgiana, were in the United States; friends and fellow writers – or 'Coscribblers' as he once signed himself – like Leigh Hunt, were near neighbours in the suburbs north of London and the nature of the letters Keats writes to them are very often determined, under-standably, by that sense of difference. Some of his letters are com-posed across a number of days; others are written at one quick sitting with the expectation of them arriving within a matter of hours. In terms of letter reading, Keats is alert to the message sent merely through the look of handwriting. It is, as he puts it in a let-ter to his sister Fanny, equivalent to reading the expression on someone's face: 'We judge of peoples hearts by their Countenances; may we not judge of Letters in the same way? if so, the Letter does not contain unpleasant news – Good or bad spirits have an effect on the handwriting' (*Letters*, II, 238).

This highly self-conscious alertness to the possibilities of letters, their peculiar relationship to self-presence and their compensation for absence between friends and relations, is captured in all its playful contradictoriness by a letter of Keats to George and Georgiana in 1819. Letters to George and Georgiana form a sig-nificant body of the surviving correspondence and, as we shall see, Keats makes great creative play out of this double audience:

> [...] – I must take an opportunity here to observe that though I am writing *to* you I am all the while writing *at* your Wife – This explana-tion will account for my speaking sometimes *hoity-toityishly*. Whereas if you were alone I should sport a little more sober sadness. I am like a squi[n]ting gentleman who saying soft things to one Lady ogles another – or what is as bad in arguing with a person on his left hand appeals with his eyes to one one the right. His Vision is elastic he bends it to a certain object but having a patent sp[r]ing it flies off. Writing has this disadvan[ta]ge of speaking. one cannot write a wink, or a nod, or a grin, or a purse of the Lips, or a *smile* – O *law*! One can-[not] put ones finger to one's nose or yerk ye in the ribs, or lay hold of your but-ton in writing – but in all the most lively and titterly parts of my Letter you must not fail to imagine me as the epic poets say – now here, now there, now with one foot pointed at the ceiling, now with another – now with my pen on my ear, now with my elbow in my mouth – O my friends you loose the action – and attitude is every thing as Fusili said when he took up his leg like a Musket to shoot a Swallow just darting behind his shoulder [...]   (*Letters*, II, 204–5)

This is typical of Keats's daring playfulness in letter-writing: the way he projects himself before his recipients in various comic identities; the way it risks being misunderstood and causing offence. It also aptly demonstrates the mixture of private humour and literary allusion ('yerk ye in the ribs', for example, is taken from Shakespeare's *Othello*). And, perhaps, most typically of all, as it draws attention to the limits of letter-writing it demonstrates an extraordinary attempt to overcome those limits by deploying an almost theatrical imagination to make the writer present to his correspondents. Bemoaning the absence of physical presence and gesture, Keats seizes the opportunity for role-playing by presenting himself in peculiarly graphic terms.

It is already evident, not least from the last extract, that Keats's letters are heavily inflected with an awareness of gender difference. In this chapter, we will focus on the different ways in which his exploration of selfhood, particularly his idea of the selfhood of the poet, is intersected by a strong and often competing awareness of gender and the dictates of a powerful sexual desire. His letters reveal a passionate and fraught engagement with gender and sexuality as they are experienced as a part of an intense network of male friendships, his location of the masculine self and sexual morality in the context of national identity, and his anxious encounters with women, including Fanny Brawne.

In what we might otherwise think of as the very straightforwardly earnest conventions of letter-writing, Keats demonstrates a peculiar degree of self-conscious playfulness. In his surviving correspondence, he usually signs himself 'very' or 'most affectionate' brother or friend, but there are occasions when he writes not as plain John, John Keats or J.K., but as 'Junkets' or 'John O'Grots'. And as if to draw attention to the strange sincerity of conventional letter-writing, he proclaims himself 'Your's unfeignedly', 'Your's if possible', 'Your affectionate Parson', and, perhaps most bizarrely, when writing to his friend the painter Benjamin Robert Haydon at a time when Egypt was fashionable, 'Your's like a Pyramid'. All these, of course, demonstrate Keats's famous capacity for humorous self-fashioning, for exploring different identities, including that of the poet. But as the brief illustrations looked at so far already indicate, Keats's exploration of self in his letters is not some free-floating, disembodied autobiographical project, but is doggedly embedded in the idea of correspondence. His famously empathetic imagination is here determinedly employed, as the quotation at the head of this chapter illustrates, in the business of reciprocation, of writing to the moment of letter-reading. Like any very good correspondent, Keats writes with an acute sense of his recipients.

I. FRIENDSHIP

His letter to Richard Woodhouse, dated 27 October 1818, is one of his most famous, for it contains his speculations on the poetical character and his idea of the 'camelion poet'. This is one of Keats's most daring explorations of selfhood, particularly of the strange selfhood of which a poet like himself is possessed. He begins by distinguishing himself from the Wordsworthian kind of poet whose ego is predominant. Identity for the sort of poet Keats is

> [...] is not itself – it has no self – it is every thing and nothing – It has no character – it enjoys light and shade; it lives in gusto, be it foul or fair, high or low, rich or poor, mean or elevated – It has as much delight in conceiving an Iago as an Imogen. What shocks the virtuous philosop[h]er, delights the camelion Poet. It does no harm from its relish of the dark side of things any more than from its taste for the bright one; because they both end in speculation. A Poet is the most unpoetical of any thing in existence; because he has no Identity – he is continually in for – and filling some other Body [...]
> (*Letters*, I, 387)

Keats embarks on dangerous territory here and flies in the face of conventional morality, especially public morality, where the idea of having a 'character' meant something much stronger than it does today. For Keats's society, to have a character was to be in possession of an achieved ethical selfhood. So, to remove oneself so emphatically from such a notion is to risk being considered immoral. And there's a sense of Keats guarding himself against such a claim by his insistence that 'it does no harm'. Although arguing for what appears to be an amoral position, Keats also runs the risk of being seriously misinterpreted by his friends. There's a real danger of a breakdown in communication if he is asking his friends to release him from the connection between what he says and who he is. He then goes on, in a surprisingly abject and apologetic vein, to explain the workings of this absence of identity in a social context:

> It is a wretched thing to confess; but is a very fact that not one word I ever utter can be taken for granted as an opinion growing out of

> my identical nature – how can it, when I have no nature? When I am
> in a room with People if I ever am free from speculating on creations
> of my own brain, then not myself goes home to myself: but the iden-
> tity of every one in the room begins to to press upon me that, I am
> in a very little time anhilated – not only among Men; it would be the
> same in a Nursery of children: I know not whether I make myself
> wholly understood: I hope enough so to let you see that no depend-
> ence is to be placed on what I said that day.   (*Letters*, I, 387)

Keats is doing his best to clear himself of a charge of misconduct –
at least of having said something irritable and upsetting. His genuine attempt to define the problematic nature of irritable genius
and the amoral pleasure in beauty which his kind of poet is fasci-
nated by is, simultaneously, an attempt to retrieve his standing with
a friend.

Rather than diminishing such a famous letter, an awareness of its
complex context should make us marvel all the more at what is
possible in an epistolary text. Keats continues to consider his poetic
ambitions and speculates on the clash between his concern for
'human affairs' and 'finer spirits', his familiar split between the real
and the ideal, but not before he signs off in half-humorous, self-
mocking fashion which has the potential to turn the idea of letter-
writing and 'yours sincerely' completely on its head:

> But even now I am perhaps not speaking from myself; but from
> some character in whose soul I now live. I am sure however that this
> next sentence is from myself. I feel your anxiety, good opinion and
> friendliness in the highest degree, and am
> > Your's most sincerely   (*Letters*, I, 388)

The letter ends – as it had begun – with the business of friendship.
Keats's daring speculations here are part of a correspondence: a
continuing debate between the two friends not only as to the character of genius, but also about what Keats has said on a previous
occasion. Even this, one of his most quoted statements about the
figure of the poet, is part of an ongoing process of definition
between friends which operates not simply on an intellectual level,
but on a level of sociability. Keats's definition of himself as a 'camelion poet' emerges as part of a necessary self-explanation between
friends for his past conduct.

Another of Keats's most quoted letters, the one to his brothers in
which he uses the phrase 'Negative Capability', also emerges from

a similar concern for sociality. Keats begins his letter with an enthusiastic account of Edmund Kean's performance in Shakespeare's *Richard III* and a visit to the Royal Academy to see pictures by the contemporary history painter Benjamin West. This eventually leads him to report on a dinner party at the house of his artist-friend Haydon in which he joined in conversation with an uncongenial group of cultured gentlemen whose talk was critical of Kean. Keats's distaste for their negative wit, as opposed to what he considers to be true humour, makes him castigate their fashionability and the certainty of their critical and moral opinions. This, in turn, leads him to write of his return from the Christmas pantomime with his friends Reynolds, Brown and Dilke. And it is in reporting his conversation with the last – what Keats tellingly describes as 'not a dispute but a disquisition' – that the famous phrase emerges:

> ... & at once it struck me, what quality went to form a Man of Achievement especially in Literature & which Shakespeare possessed so enormously – I mean *Negative Capability*, that is when man is capable of being in uncertainties, Mysteries, doubts, without any irritable reaching after fact & reason – (*Letters*, I, 193)

The earlier parts of the letter which deal with Kean's acting of Shakespeare and Keats's revulsion at fashionable wit lead towards this famous definition of Shakespearian creativity which critics have used so frequently to define Keats's own genius. As with the previous example of the 'camelion poet', such famous speculations emerge from an acutely felt social context, a context of the company of men in which the nature of friendship is to debate kinds of genius. And, as Keats's significant qualification indicates, it might very often be difficult to distinguish between a dispute and an earnest disquisition, something to which Keats and his friends seem to have been particularly prone. Keats's 'Man of Achievement', possessed of the quality of 'Negative Capability', is defined precisely against the men of wit and easy moral censure who appear early in the letter and it is refined in a precarious process of debate between friends which, because of its vehemence, is capable of putting even such friendship in jeopardy.

Keats's letters, then, might best be read as performances of the self in which, as the quotation above indicates, the writer's own anticipation of their reception – both by his correspondents

and, importantly, beyond them – plays a significant role, occasionally surfacing to form the very content of a letter. Keats performs
for his friends and family, for himself, and for posterity in these
excitingly multidirectional texts. The main point I wish to establish, though, is that these peculiarly creative acts of writing are
complexly mediated by relationships, and the acts of daring self-
definition which famously take place within them are an integrated
part of correspondence: acts of self-articulation which are crucially
dependent on those others who will receive the letter. Even when
Keats is, it seems, experimenting with letter-writing in a most solipsistic or self-regarding way in such textual circumstances, it can
never be an uninterrupted narcissism which takes place. The sense
of communication, expedition, and reception must always obtrude
upon the egocentric experiment and turn it towards the gaze of
another.

At the other extreme, there are examples in the correspondence
where Keats engages with letter-writing as a shared experience: his
own contribution spliced with those of a friend on the same sheet of
paper. One such occurs on a trip to Bedhampton with his friend
Charles Brown. This shared or split letter clearly provides Keats with
a slightly different set of playful possibilities and raises its own questions about the representation of self within his correspondence:

> I am sorry – that Brown and you are getting so very witty – my
> modest feathered Pen frizzles like baby roast beef at making its
> entrance among such tantrum sentences – or rather ten senses.
> Brown *super* or *supper* sirnamed the Sleek has been getting thinner
> a little by pining opposite Miss Muggins [...] Miss M. has persuaded
> Brown to shave his Whiskers – he came down to Breakfast like the
> Sign of the full Moon – his Profile is quite alter'd – He looks more
> like an oman than I ever could think it possible – and on putting on
> M^{rs} D's Callash the deception was complete especially as his voice
> is trebbled by making love in the draught of a door way – I too am
> metamorphosed – a young oman here in Bed—hampton has over
> persuaded me to wear my Shirtcollar up to my eyes. Mrs Snook I
> catch smoking it every now and then and I believe Brown does –
> but I cannot now look sideways – Brown wants to scribble more so
> I will finish with a marginal note – Viz – Remember me to
> Wentworth Place and Elm Cottage – not forgetting Millamant –
> Your's if possible J—Keats– [...]   (*Letters*, II, 35–6)

The letter continues in Brown's hand before being interrupted by
Keats so that by the end they are, in effect, performing a double-act.

Keats's contribution is italicised:

> This is abominable! I did but go up stairs to put on a clean &
> starched hand-kerchief, & that over weening rogue read my letter &
> scrawled over one of my sheets, *and given him a counterpain, –*
> I wish I could blank-it all over *and beat him with a certain rod,*
> and have a fresh one bolstered up. *Ah! He may dress me as he likes*
> *but he shan't ticlke me pillow the feathers,* – I would not give a tester
> for such puns, *let us ope brown will go no further in the Bedroom &*
> not call Mat Snook a relation to Matt-rass – *This is grown to a*
> *conclusion – I had excellent puns in my head but one bad one from*
> *Brown has quite upset me* but I am quite set-up for more, but I'm
> content to be conqueror. Your's in love, Ch[as] Brown.
> N.B. *I beg leaf to withdraw all my Puns – they are all wash, an*
> *base uns –* (Letters, II, 36)

Such a letter provides ample evidence of Keats's propensity for
bawdy playfulness. The profusion of puns moves quickly towards
the bedroom and a rather saucy set of double entendres, including
'rod' for penis and 'feathers' for female pubic hair. In terms of identity and self-fashioning, it indicates a willingness to submerge one's
identity, if temporarily. Here Keats is merged grammatically, at
least, as he becomes a part of Brown's sentences. More particularly,
for the purpose of this study, the letter also establishes a ground of
homosocial bonding for this merging to take place. The two relatively young men dare not only to share the usually intimate space
of a letter, but also to represent each other in relation to fashion
and love. The terms in which they do so are indicative of a major
strand in Keats's letters: their exploration of identity, gender, and
romance in the context of male friendship. The two young men
mock each other and themselves for changes in their appearance
brought about by the impact of women on them. Thus, Keats treats
the shaving off of Brown's whiskers as a kind of emasculation or
unmanning articulated in an explicitly self-conscious language of
gender difference. With the removal of his masculinising facial hair,
Brown, already diminished through pining, is now transformed,
according to Keats, into an 'oman': Keats's term for a woman,
where woman is defined through lack as a kind of 'nothing-man'.
And Keats includes himself in the process of feminised diminution
as he gives us a graphic example of a rather literal self-effacement:
his shirt collar worn up to hide his eyes. Even more daring is his
idea of beating Brown with his 'rod' and imagining 'dressing him'

but not allowing him to progress beyond his 'feathers'. There's an interesting cross-gender substitution going on here. The heterosexual actions of Brown and Keats are teasingly transposed on themselves and their mocking relationship with each other.

What takes place is a parodic testing-out of the limits of masculine identity ostensibly at the hands of women, but more immediately through the pens of the two young men. As they write themselves as the supposed victims of love – love-lorn suitors doing what female admirers ask of them – they confirm the terms of their superior masculinity in this game of supposed feminisation. Even Keats's opening to his part of the letter draws attention to this risqué ritual of punning as a testing-out of his masculine identity. The reference to his 'modest feathered Pen frizzl[ing] like baby roast beef' provides a tantalising image of youthful English masculinity preparing itself for the hot stuff of romance.

A similar deployment of bawdy humour in conjunction with Brown occurs in a letter of 1818 to his brother Tom when Keats quotes – or at least attributes to Brown – the following punning play on place-names:

> Cairn-something July 17th-
> My dear Tom,
>   Here's Brown going on so that I cannot bring to Mind how the two last days have vanished – for example he says 'The Lady of the Lake went to Rock herself to sleep on Arthur's seat and the Lord of the Isles coming to Press a Piece and seeing her Assleap remembered their last meeting at Corry stone Water so touching her with one hand on the Vallis Lucis while he other un-Derwent her White-haven, Ireby stifled her clack man on, that he might her Anglesea and give her a Buchanan and said.' I told you last how we were stared at in Glasgow – [...]   (*Letters*, I, 333–4)

As Robert Gittings has pointed out,[2] this quoted material is full of contemporary sexual slang: 'Water' meaning semen; 'stone', for testes; 'Vallis Lucis' and 'haven', the female pudenda; and 'stifled', meaning sexually occupied; as well as some more obvious ones still familiar today. This has all the hallmarks of the retelling of a dirty joke amongst young men – a learnt, self-contained set-piece with which to open the letter to his brother in entertaining fashion. As with the earlier Bedhampton example, there is a self-cancelling (or at least self-regulating) aspect to Keats's use of bawdy. Like his admission in the other case that his puns are 'base'uns' (basins), here he distances himself by placing the responsibility for the joke on Brown. In both cases, Keats displays some degree of anxiety or unease which often goes along with punning and, one might add, punning of such a ribald nature. But Keats remains silent about his response to what he presents as Brown's bawdiness. Brown's 'going on so' is related to his own inability to recount the adventures of the last two days and one is left wondering whether the friend's inveterate joking is helping to pass the time or simply acts as an irritating interference with the process of memory.

What such examples clearly illustrate is the degree to which Keats's letters are deeply involved in a shared process of self-definition and self-presentation between men. The Bedhampton letter is a good example of Keats's continued interest in role-playing, dressing-up, and the trying out of different versions of a masculine self. Like Brown, he too had once grown fashionable whiskers, had briefly flirted with Byronic costume, and had also kitted himself out in sea-faring costume.[3] How one might look, be looked at, and present oneself, are, unsurprisingly, a major part of Keats's correspondence. And as these examples also show, Keats is acutely aware of the gender of the onlooker. What happens before the male gaze – even the gaze of the letter as it were – is strongly defined in his writing, as we have already seen in the poetry. Just as some of his most famous poems are concerned with the power of desirous looking – as in 'Ode to Psyche', 'The Eve of St Agnes', and 'Lamia' – so his letters are conceived as opportunities to present oneself, though absent, to the gaze of others. The empathetic imagination which allows him to speculate and second-guess the mood of his recipients also allows him, at times, an almost theatrical, creative power of self-presentation.

One of the best examples of the nature of Keats's idea of friendship and its connection with the business of poetry is his letter to friend and fellow poet John Hamilton Reynolds, dated 21 September 1817. At this time, Keats was staying with Benjamin Bailey, another friend, in Oxford, in an attempt to progress with the writing of *Endymion* and the letter seems to have been written to Reynolds in order to maintain the relationship, to rekindle ideas of a group of friends, and to receive and convey news of the others. The letter is particularly revealing for the way in which it negotiates and exploits the complex movement between the individuated friendship of two men and that of the group. It provides a good illustration of how Keats's mockery, his teasing, allows him to explore the boundary between the homosocial and the homoerotic. Perhaps most importantly, it shows Keats exploring new territory simultaneously: the testing and teasing out of new forms of poetry and friendship go hand in hand. Although it does not announce itself as such, of course, this letter provides a striking example of one of the routes by which Keats was about to set out on a voyage to discover new kinds of love and love poetry.

It begins with a humorous attack on his correspondent which employs exaggerated theatrical allusions of physical combat. 'So you are determined to be my mortal foe – draw a Sword at me, and I will forgive – Put a Bullet in my Brain, and I will shake it out as a dewdrop from the Lion's Mane; – put me on a Gridiron, and I will fry with great complancency – but, oh horror! to come upon me in the shape of a Dun! Send me Bills!' (Letters, I, 162). If Reynolds is to be his enemy, then Keats is willing to undergo any kind of physical torture, but he will not accept his friend forwarding bills to him. The opening gambit of the letter establishes its grounds of male friendship around an ethics of partiality which fends off the usual social constraints. Friendship defines itself against money and the workings of the everyday economy. It also immediately presents such friendship as precarious. For all the mockery and theatrical pretence, there's always a chance of it turning into enmity and even physical antagonism, particularly over the fraught business of money loans. Such mock antagonism also provides a suitable corrective or defence mechanism for the intimacy which is to follow. Keats goes on to describe the activities he has been enjoying in Oxford and immediately risks a reference to Reynolds's body. The streams of Oxford are 'more in number than your eye lashes', he observes. It immediately becomes apparent that the letter performs and commemorates Keats's making his friend present during his absence. And this becomes quite explicit when the letter informs us that the two friends in Oxford, enjoying themselves on the river Isis, have 'christened' 'one particularly nice nest' as 'Reynolds's Cove', a place where they may talk 'as may be' and read Wordsworth. Having established a place and a presence for Reynolds, Keats proceeds to visualise Hunt and Reynolds together in 'the Pit' back in London. Next, he characteristically defines himself against Wordsworth, proclaiming himself to be one who definitely does 'delight to season [his] fireside with personal talk', a propensity he refers to engagingly as a 'little itch that way'. Once again, the language of desire obtrudes itself upon friendship. The distinction made between Keats the Cockney poet of the chatty hearth and Wordsworth's cold, northern self-containment also operates on a political level. Keats clearly finds a kind of democratic levelling in friendship; he tells his friend that he rejoices in the failings of the men he comes to know. 'They bring us to a Level', he explains. What's more, he adds (to clinch the point about warm camaraderie), the 'makes-up are very good' (*Letters*, I, 163).

This progressively more bonded and intimate trajectory of the letter is then interrupted as he moves to an attack on women writers who as 'a set of Devils', he informs Reynolds, have 'vexed and teased' England 'within the last thirty years'. The attack on the misplaced ambition and gender decorum of women writers gives way to relief when Keats informs his friend that the kind of 'real feminine modesty' that should prevail in these matters is to be found in the poetry of Katherine Philips (1631–64). Tellingly, Philips is referred to by Keats as 'one beautiful Mrs Philips' and 'the matchless Orinda' – as she was traditionally called. The woman writer, like woman more generally for Keats, exists on two levels: that of conventional social reality and that of the realm of romance. The gap between the two is often jarring, as it is here, but Keats can use it to sharp, creative effect. Keats's letter then quotes at length Katherine Philips's poem 'To Mrs M. A. at Parting', in which she describes the elemental love between friends as a passionate exchange or mingling of souls. In stanza nine of the poem this new kind of relationship is described as 'teaching the world new love': it will 'redeem the age and sex'. Although the poem is offered up from one poet to another on the grounds of its aesthetic qualities, it also clinches the friendship motive of the letter, a function which Keats highlights by a significant gloss. After the lines: 'She that would be Rosania's friend, / Must be at least compleat', he adds: 'A compleat friend – this Line sounded very oddly to me at first' (*Letters*, I, 165). In a daring act of revealed intimacy, Keats exposes his process of thought about friendship and indirectly offers a fine compliment to his recipient. Beyond the personal dynamic, it also illustrates the extent to which Keats is here thinking through the nature of friendship, its level of commitment and its limits.

Immediately after this daring quotation and annotation, he returns to the safer realm of homosocial camaraderie by asking after their other friends Haydon, Rice, Martin and Hazlitt. He reports on his progress with *Endymion*, exchanges greetings from his brothers, and finally asks for some stanzas so that he and Bailey may read them in 'Reynolds's cove'. Keats uses Philips's poem to further his own attempt to 'redeem the age and sex'; that is to say, he is clearly self-conscious in his quest to redefine the nature of male friendship and does so in the context of national identity.

This letter performs friendship at a number of levels, most adventurously through the medium of poetic quotation where a seventeenth-century poem proclaiming the intense and passionate friendship love between two women can be used to consolidate male friendship love. Typically, the letter proceeds subtly and indirectly. It moves through apparent oppositions or conflicts: Reynolds is a mock enemy at the beginning and women writers are initially a threat before being safely accommodated to provide a model for male bonding. Male friendship proceeds through a process of defence, a naming of the opposition, in this case money and women. Keats's idea of friendship is clearly pitted against the workings of commercial society, and, as we shall see, against the idea of fashion in which he situates women. Gendered identity negatively determined by an economy of fashion is one of the recurring motives of Keats's letters and explains the hostility very often generated in them towards both women and the male figure of the dandy.

Even one of Keats's most famous letters – the one he sent to Benjamin Bailey dated 22 November 1817 – provides a dramatic understanding of the precarious nature of friendship and of how that friendship actually provides the motive for many of his most famous definitions of the nature of the poetic self. This letter has been the object of extended and intense critical scrutiny because of its expression of the nature of genius and identity embodied in such phrases as 'the holiness of the heart's affections' and 'O for a life of Sensations' – as well as Keats's ability to 'take part in the existence of a sparrow' and 'live for the Moment'. It begins as a reassurance to Bailey after a falling out with another friend in their circle, Haydon. The subsequent explanation proffered by Keats about the nature of identity and genius which leads on to an analysis of his own nature in this regard, begins as a way of dealing with the conflicted, agitated and precarious nature of this rather special group of friends.

Anxiety is the order of the day here, most frequently registered by one of Keats's favourite words: 'teased'. For Keats, this seems to mean the opposite of ease – more like an agitated unease. Having no identity is, at one level, a convenient means of by-passing the conventional ethics of friendship and letter-writing. One clearly gets the sense that the boundaries of conventional friendship are being expanded. Imagining a new kind of friendship and how to cope with its precariousness and fractiousness is an integral part of the project to redefine the identity or personality of genius and the new ethical codes of conduct which must be suffered and experienced in its wake. Keats's constructive advice to Bailey that such a vitriolic response from Haydon goes with the territory of such a genius is followed by his own admission not only of extreme response on occasion, but also of a less expected admission of insensibility. This is a truly negative insensitivity – completely unlike the famously celebrated 'Negative Capability' which allows him (by way of compensation) to take part in the existence of a sparrow. Having reflected on the nature of 'Worldly Happiness', Keats's letter takes a more personal turn:

> I look not for it if it be not in the present hour – nothing startles me beyond the Moment. The setting sun will always set me to rights – or if a Sparrow come before my Window I take part in its existince and pick about the Gravel. The first thing that strikes me on hea[r]ing a Misfortune having befalled another is this. 'Well it cannot be helped. – he will have the pleasure of trying the resourses of his spirit, and I beg now my dear Bailey that hereafter should you observe any thing cold in me not to but it to the account of heartlessness but abstraction – for I assure you I sometimes feel not the influence of a Passion or Affection during a whole week – and so long this sometimes continues I begin to suspect myself and the genuiness of my feelings at other times – thinking them a few barren Tragedy-tears – [...]   (*Letters*, I, 186)

This fascinating letter teases out the connection between living in the moment and the realm of imagination. It measures the experience of being troubled by quarrels against a studied abstraction. Keats's own response to Bailey could be seen as a negotiation, a warning of his own difficult personality. It also suggests that there's a conflict between these realms for Keats: whether to inhabit the present or go beyond it, just as the central part of the letter juggles with the truth of imagination and the possibility of an afterlife.

Keats's letter to Bailey, then, is designed to make the peace, to palliate his correspondent's current disgruntlement, but also to place such a friction in the context of philosophical debate. The extent to which one exists in and is 'teased' by the world is an integral part of Keats's aesthetic explorations, not simply an irritating distraction. His statement midway through the letter that 'I am continually running away from the subject – sure this cannot be exactly the case with a complex Mind – one that is imaginative and at the same time careful of its fruits', nicely dramatises the point. While it articulates a healthy degree of self-doubt, it demonstrates how a letter can best capture the movement of a mind as it apparently 'runs away' from its ostensible subject. It suggests that such movement is not actual digression, but connection; and that apparent failure to stick to the point is, in fact, a kind of complex connection. The peculiarity of the self he projects to his friend can easily be underestimated. His propensity to 'take part in the existence' of a sparrow 'and pick about the Gravel' has all too easily been read as a sign of his empathetic, protean creativity in which the chameleon nature of the poet takes on the identity of other things. Perhaps the strangest aspect of this propensity as articulated here in its full context is its casualness, its being a confession of the degree to which he is dictated to by the moment. In conventional moral terms (and the terms which might be thought of as applying in friendship), to admit to such an easy falling in with the present might be thought to militate against morality or at least the usual expectations of sensitivity. Keats revels in a kind of ethical callousness, an emotional insensitivity which completely fails to imagine or empathise with the problems his friend has written to him about. This is an interesting inversion of the man of feeling often associated in the literature of sensibility with the figure of the poet. Keats constructs his version of the man of genius or poet as a creature of insensibility. In this respect, the truly daring aspect of this letter to a friend is, perhaps, the way it can speculate even about the very genuineness of his feelings, albeit in bouts of emotional blankness which he admits last only for a week.

II. NATIONAL IDENTITY

The fraught homosocially bonded friendships which are established and tested out in Keats's letters are defined against and supported by more general assumptions about masculinity. For the post-Waterloo Britain of Keats's time masculinity was to a considerable degree integrated with a national identity. This, in turn, is often vigorously and aggressively set off against foreign, particularly

French, forms of masculinity which are seen as dangerously effeminate. And in the post-war period in which Keats is reaching maturity there is considerable debate about the national character and its appropriate masculinity, particularly on the perceived threat of it relaxing into a more refined, less robust form with the progress of an increasingly polite and refined culture.

One of the most explicit instances of this sense of gendered national identity manifesting itself in his correspondence occurs in a letter to Benjamin Bailey written when Keats was enjoying a short stay at Teignmouth in Devon. He writes from a sense of general frustration and thwarted activity in which he questions his ability as a reasoner or philosopher and reflects negatively on his argumentative and passionate temper. This also extends to include a severe questioning of the nature of reality and the force of poetry. Nagging doubt as to the power of his chosen vocation leads him to think of 'Poetry itself [as] a mere Jack a lanthern' and his disillusionment focuses on what he characteristically sees as the prevailing and pervasive commercial spirit of the age: 'every thing is worth what it will fetch, so probably every mental pursuit takes its reality and worth from the ardour of the pursuer – being in itself a nothing.' Frustration of a poetic and sexual kind are at one here:

> [...] by the by you may say what you will of devonshire: the thuth is, it is a splashy, rainy, misty snowy, foggy, haily floody, muddy, slipshod County – the hills are very beautiful, when you get a sight of 'em – the Primroses are out, but then you are in – the Cliffs are of a fine deep Colour, but then the Clouds are continually vieing with them – The Women like your London People in a sort of negative way – because the native men are the poorest creatures in England – because Government never have thought it worth while to send a recruiting party among them. When I think of Wordswo[r]th's Sonnet 'Vanguard of Liberty! ye Men of Kent!' the degenerated race about me are Pulvis Ipecac. Simplex a strong dose – Were I a Corsair I'd make a descent on the South Coast of Devon, if I did not run the chance of having Cowardice imputed to me: as for the Men they'd run away into the methodist meeting houses, and the Women would be glad of it – Had England been a large devonshire we should not have won the Battle of Waterloo – There are knotted oaks – there are lusty rivulets there are Meadows such as are not – there are vallies of femminine Climate – but there are no thews and Sinews – Moore's Almanack is here a curiosity – A[r]ms Neck and shoulders may at least be<e> seen there, and The Ladies read it as some out of the way romance – Such a quelling Power have these thoughts

over me, that I fancy the very Air of a deteriorating quality. [...] A
Devonshirer standing on his native hills is not a distinct object – he
does not show against the light – a wolf or two would dispossess
him. I like, I love England, I like its strong Men – Give me a 'long
brown plain' for my Morning so I may meet with some of Edmond
Iron side's desendents – Give me a barren mould so I may meet with
some shadowing of Alfred in the shape of a Gipsey, a Huntsman or
as Shepherd. Scenery is fine – but human nature is finer – [...]
Homer is very fine, Achilles is fine, Diomed is fine, Shakspeare is
fine, Hamlet is fine, Lear is fine, but dwindled englishmen are not
fine [...]   (*Letters*, I, 241–2)

A letter ostensibly about mounting frustration and irritation at the
wet spring weather develops into a fascinating attack on the Devon
landscape and its male inhabitants. Keats reveals himself to be possessed of a strong sense of masculine Englishness. Like many others of his time, his definition of the national character is strongly
informed by the military experience of the war with France for the
best part of two decades. Male prowess is measured by the defeat
of Napoleon at Waterloo. In this instance, Keats berates the men of
Devon for their lack of military suitability. This troubled sense of
English masculinity combines with his distaste for the topographical. A disturbing historical sense also clouds his thought as his dis-
satisfaction with the present is haunted by the literary as well as the
military past. Alongside his apparent aggression towards his fellow
Devonshire men is a characteristic predatory desire as far as the
Devonshire women are concerned. Keats's tirade against the 'dwindled men' of the county is matched by a roving desire for their
women which even takes the form of a tentative imagining of himself as a raiding Byronic Corsair. There's also a strange transposition of body to landscape. By the end of the letter, the aggression
towards the inadequacy of contemporary masculinity imagined in
terms of physical, corporeal power begins to look like a reaching
after certainty, a physical definiteness which can be played off
against the more ethereal and speculative life of the mind.

Keats's berating of contemporary English masculinity forms an
integral part of his anxious questioning of his own aesthetics.
Assuring himself that his real concern is 'human nature', Keats
begins to query just what substance or manifestation such 'nature'
has in the world. As he removes himself from the topographical or
landscape school of poets in order to focus on human passion, so
his acute sense of his own scepticism seems to remove him from the

realm of the philosophical or merely rational. But, clearly, the kind of passionate intensity of the body with which he seems inevitably to be engaged is distinctly unhappy and disappointed with the contemporary models it sees before it. Keats is weighing up the relative reality of the passion and character he is interested in. Can it be seen walking the soggy fields of England or can it only exist in the realm of imagination and romance? In this letter at least, there's a conjuring of historical versions of masculinity which traverse the familiar contexts of classical literature and the English Civil War. There's a strong political inflection to Keats's bemoaning the current state of the men of England here: a republican tradition reaching from the ancients through Cromwell to Wordsworth's sonnet on liberty.

A letter written from Scotland during his walking-tour with Brown illustrates the degree to which Keats also conceived of femininity – or, at least, the position of women – in similarly national terms. In this instance, though, his concern is with the prevailing institutionalised system of religious morals artificially enforcing a miserable state of femininity in the lower ranks rather than a gendered national identity. Keats's unorthodox religious views and his antagonism towards organised religion are here at their most vehement alongside his strongly developed sense of social progress. Intersecting problematically with these more abstracted views is the same kind of frustrated would-be predatory desire evident in the letter from *Teignmouth*. The immediate object of his anger, however, is the joyless morality of the Scottish Kirk:

> [...] I can perceive a great difference in the nations from the Chambermaid at this nate Inn kept by Mr Kelly – She is fair, kind and ready to laugh, because she is out of the horrible dominion of the Scotch kirk – A Scotch Girl stands in terrible awe of the Elders – poor little Susannas – They will scarcely laugh – they are greatly to be pitied and the kirk is greatly to be damn'd. These kirkmen have [...] made Men, Women, Old Men Young Men old Women, young women boys, girls and infants all careful – so that they are formed into regular Phalanges of savers and gainers – such a thrifty army cannot fail to enrich their Country and give it a greater apperance of comfort than that of their poor irish neighbours – These kirkmen have done Scotland harm – they have banished puns and laughing and kissing (except in cases where the very danger and crime must make it very fine and gustful. I shall make a full stop at kissing for after that there should be a better paren*t*hesis: and go on to remind you of the fate of Burns. [...] how sad it is when a luxurious imagination is obliged in self defence to deaden its delicacy in

vulgarity, and riot in thing[s] attainable that it may not have leisure
to go mad after thing[s] which are not [...] It is true that out of suf-
france there is no greatness, no dignity; that in the most abstracted
Pleasure there is no lasting happiness: yet who would not like to discover over again that Cleopatra was a Gipsey, Helen a Rogue and
Ruth a deep one? [...] Were the fingers made to squeeze a guinea or
a white hand? Were the lips made to hold a pen or a kiss? [...] The
present state of society demands this and this convinces me that the
world is very young and in a verry ignorant state – We live in a bar-
barous age. I would sooner be a wild deer than a Girl under the
dominion of the kirk, and I would sooner be a wild hog than
be the occasion of a Poor Creatures pennance before those execrable
elders [...]   (*Letters*, I, 319–20)

Keats ruminates on the prevailing morality of Lowland Scottish
society and its effect on his own propensity to engage with the
young women of its lower orders. Even here, of course, the figure
of the poet (in this case Robert Burns) weighs significantly in the
balance. Keats's homosocial realm of bawdy is constituted as 'puns
and laughing and kissing' – the very kind of fun prohibited by the
Kirk. Scotland's combination of strictly enforced morality and
thriftiness is a particularly deadening combination for Keats and
this leads him into the opposite kind of historical schema he
applied to the men of Devon. There he deployed a narrative of
diminution: a falling away from the heroic past, even the very
recent heroic past of Waterloo. Here the historical view is one of
progress as he delights in describing the tight morality of the Kirk
as a form of barbarism. His conjuring of a state of nature in
response to this – his preference for the identity of deer rather than
a young Scottish girl in this system and his preference for being
a 'wild hog' rather than the lover who brings her into disrepute –
while it speaks of a laudable desire to be liberated from such a
repressive sexual morality, also contains a disturbing force of
a thwarted libertinism. Our response to such a letter is likely to be
fraught: some identification and sympathy with Keats's almost
Lawrentian castigation of the repressed morality of the Kirk; distaste perhaps for his articulation of a frustrated roving male desire
with its predatory instinct focused on serving girls.

III. WOMEN

We have already seen how Keats's commentaries on the men of
Devon and Scottish working-class women extend to a sense of

gendered national identity and are informed by discourses of historical progress and economics. In those instances, Keats seems to possess a clear sense of social realities, even if these are measured unfavourably in each case against a heroic classical antiquity and a state of nature. In many of his commentaries on women this comparative sense is composed of a mythic idealism on the one hand and a cynical, even disappointed, realism on the other. For Keats, the figure of woman is troubling and disturbing precisely because she inhabits, in his mind, this anxious dichotomy.

In a number of his letters to Benjamin Bailey this disturbed idea of woman is brought to a surprising and daring degree of articulation, Keats even going so far as to recognise it as a problem which might not only create difficulties with his relationship with women, but also endanger his relationships with male friends and relations. In one letter he refers back to a question of Bailey's concerning 'why must women suffer'. This is later taken up by Keats in a brief shorthand reference to 'women suffering from cancers' before the topic surfaces in a letter of July 1818 written in Scotland while on his walking tour with Brown. Coming towards the end of the journey, he is forced to contemplate a return to 'Society' and, in particular, his renewed acquaintance with the Reynolds family, including their two young daughters. This unappealing prospect leads him into the particularly revealing and surprisingly candid account of his problem with women which we examined in chapter 1:

> I am certain I have not a right feeling towards Women – at this moment I am striving to be just to them but I cannot – Is it because they fall so far beneath my Boyish imagination? When I was a Schoolboy I though[t] a fair Woman a pure Goddess, my mind was a soft nest in which some one of them slept though she knew it not – I have no right to expect more than their reality. I thought them ethereal above Men – I find then perhaps equal – great by comparison is very small – Insult may be inflicted in more ways than by Word or action – one who is tender of being insulted does not like to think an insult against another – I do not like to think insults in a Lady's Company – I commit a Crime with her which absence would have not known – Is it not extraordinary? When among Men I have no evil thoughts, no malice, no spleen – I feel free to speak or to be silent – I can listen and from every one I can learn – my hands are in my pockets I am free from all suspicion and comfortable. When I am among Women I have evil thoughts, malice spleen – I cannot speak or be silent – I am full of Suspicions and therefore listen to no thing – I am in a hurry to be gone – You must be charitable and put all this perversity to my being disappointed since Boyhood [...] I must

absolutely get over this – but how? The only way is to find the root
of evil, and so cure it 'with backward mutters of dissevering Power'.
That is a difficult thing; for an obstinate Prejudice can seldom be produced but from a gordian complication of feelings, which must take
time to unravell<ed> and care to keep unravelled – I could say a
good deal about this but I will leave it in hopes of better and more
worthy dispositions – and also content that I am wronging no one,
for after all I do think better of Womankind than to suppose they
care whether Mister John Keats five feet hight likes them or not.

(*Letters*, I, 341–2)

Keats reveals a good deal to his friend here and goes a good way to
diagnose himself with the recognition that it is pathological: something he 'must absolutely get over', an 'obstinate Prejudice' and
'evil'. He also shows what we like to think of as a peculiarly
modern awareness of the difficulty of curing himself of such a 'gordian' complex. The problem is articulated as stemming from disappointment, the product of a 'Boyish imagination', or inclination
to idealise, which means that, when faced with real women, he
can't cope with the sense of diminution or loss. To this extent, one
might be tempted to read it as a problem of growing up (or not
growing up): Keats should adjust by developing a 'Manly imagination'. This rather familiar and relatively straightforward develop-
mental narrative is complicated, however, by the sense that Keats
still inhabits the 'Boyish' version of that creative faculty, and that
when disappointment reappears in the passage it is not only still
pertinent, but now significantly loaded by its signalling his lack of
sexual or romantic experience, something exacerbated by the acute
sensitivity to his height at the end of the passage. Even the profession of doing right by women in the tentative – 'I find then perhaps
equal' – turns out to be a marred misprision.

Worst of all, Keats's admission of a self silently provoked into
malevolence by the presence of women goes beyond even the most
excruciating agonies of youthful embarrassment. What Keats
describes here is a transformation or metamorphosis of the male
self into a figure of self-loathing malevolence. The comparison with
his more celebrated capacities to engage in the empathetic workings of the 'camelion poet' and 'negative capability' is telling. The
scenario is very similar. Keats imagines himself in a room with people and, being a poet of the kind he defines himself as, finds that,
freed from Wordsworthian ego, he takes on the identities that surround him whether they be 'Men' or children. But, clearly, not

when those identities are women. What is particularly striking in the passage is the degree to which Keats is self-legislating. All of the 'behaviour' he refers to is secret. His crimes and misdemeanours are all in the mind and most probably invisible to his companions, yet Keats accords them the reality of speech or actions and does use the word 'crimes'. His tortured admission that he 'does not like to think insults in the presence of lady' reveals a continuation of the 'Boyish imagination' in which women are not to be treated equally, but deferentially. Even his use of the quotation from Milton's *Comus* to articulate his cure – ' ... backward mutters of dissevering Power' – only adds to the disturbed sense of gender identity. Though it's offered as a handy and suitably literary way of expressing the breaking of an evil spell, the context in which it appears in Milton's masque concerns the release of the virginal Lady from the entranced state in which she has been imprisoned by Comus.

The state of anxious, embittered, suspicion mixed with embarrassment and self-loathing which Keats articulates is certainly not the prevailing condition in which he represents his encounters with women in his letters. As one might expect, such a complex response generates a rich variety of representations which creatively explore this state of anxiety structured on the gap between real women and the ideal, ethereal creatures represented to his 'Boyish imagination'.

Only three months after his revealing admission of a problem with women to his friend Bailey, Keats wrote to his brother George and his wife Georgiana about his encounter with a female cousin of the Reynolds sisters at their house in London, a young woman named Jane Cox. We examined this briefly in the introduction, but can now explore it with a more complicated sense of how it works in the context of a letter. With typical literary self-consciousness Keats introduces the subject by stating 'Now I am coming the Richardson'. Invoking the eighteenth-century novelist Samuel Richardson immediately mobilises a detailed awareness of conduct combined with the presence of a threatening libertinism. Here, instead of an all too candid account of his own pathology, Keats confidently exults in his appreciation of woman as exotic object:

> She is not a Cleopatra; but she is at least a Charmian. She has a rich eastern look; she has fine eyes and fine manners. When she comes into a room she makes an impression the same as the Beauty of a Leopardess. She is too fine and too concious of her Self to repulse any Man who may address her – from habit she thinks that nothing

particular. I always find myself more at ease with such a woman; the picture before me always gives me a life and animation which I cannot possibly feel with any thing inferiour – I am at such times too much occupied in admiring to be awkward or on a tremble. I forget myself entirely because I live in her. You will by this time think I am in love with her; so before I go any further I will tell you I am not – she kept me awake one Night as a tune of Mozart's might do – I speak of the thing as a passtime and an amuzement than which I can feel none deeper than a conversation with an imperial woman the very 'yes' and 'no' of whose Lips is to me a Banquet. I dont cry to take the moon home with me in my Pocket not do I fret to leave her behind me. I like her and her like because one has no *sensations* – what we both are is taken for granted – You will suppose I have by this had much talk with her – no such thing – there are the Miss Reynoldses on the look out – they think I dont admire her because I did not stare at her – They call her a flirt to me – What a want of knowledge? She walks across a room in such a manner that a Man is drawn towards her with a magnetic Power. This they call flirting! they do not know things. They do not know what a Woman is. I believe tho' she has faults – the same as Charmian and Cleopatra might have had – Yet she is a fine thing speaking in a wordly way: for there are two distinct tempers of mind in which we judge of things – the wordly, theatrical and pantomimical; and the unearthly, spiritual and etherial – in the former Buonaparte, Lord Byron and this Charmian hold the first place in our Minds [...] As a Man in the world I love the rich talk of a Charmian; as an eternal Being I love the thought of you. I should like her to ruin me, and I should like you to save me. Do not think my dear Brother from this that my Passions are head long or likely to be ever of any pain to you – no

'I am free from Men of Pleasure's cares
By dint of feelings far more deep than theirs'

This is Lord Byron, and is one of the finest things he has said [...]
(*Letters*, I, 395–6)

In contrast to the previous letter, Keats revels confidently in a woman who answers his need for feminine idealisation, an idealisation which, if we take him at his word, helpfully, perhaps disingenuously, removes him from the anxiety of sexual involvement. Faced with such an object, Keats claims to lose his disempowering self-consciousness and is once more the projective, empathetic 'camelion poet'.

Within the passage as whole, of course, the Reynolds sisters now play the role of the irritating, superficial, fickle femininity of social reality. This other young woman whose name is tellingly omitted becomes a Charmian or Charmina. Keats revels in the superiority of, as he thinks, rising above the level of sexuality – whether it be the flirting of the sisters or the concern of his brother. The claim is that his aestheticisation of woman and his profession of a comfortable pleasure in her presence has released or liberated him from such conventional expectations. From this lofty – even ethereal eminence – Keats feels able to turn the category of woman against the sisters. It is now his possession: 'They do not know what a Woman is.' This is immediately followed by a powerful reiteration of the categories which might have been thought to be the cause of his problem with women in the earlier letter to Bailey: 'the worldly, theatrical, and pantomimical' on the one hand, the spiritual and ethereal on the other. Interestingly, in this instance, the Charmian figure still only inhabits the former, as does Lord Byron whom Keats revealingly uses for support at the end of this passage. (That he is the authority quoted when announcing his freedom from 'men of Pleasure's cares' might seem rather ironic.) The ultimate use of the categories turns out to be a confirmation of his more spiritual love for his brother which exists as an eternal idea.

A similar negotiation between woman as aestheticised object and as object of desire coupled with Keats's defensive protestations of his removal from the business of sexual attraction takes place in a letter detailing his encounter with Isabella Jones. Keats first met this rather mysterious woman in Hastings the year before and she seems to have been influential in suggesting to him the idea of 'The Eve of St Agnes' while Gittings also claims her as the subject behind Keats's famous sonnet 'Bright Star':[4]

> [...] I have met with that same Lady again [...] It was in a street which goes from Bedford Row to Lamb's Conduit Street – I passed her and turrned back – she seemed glad of it; glad to see me and not offended at my passing her before We walked on towards Islington where we called on a friend of her's who keeps a Boarding School. She has always been an enigma to me – she has <new> been in a Room with you and with Reynolds and wishes we should be acquainted without any of our common acquaintance knowing it. As we went along, some times through shabby, sometimes through decent Street[s] I had my guessing at work, not knowing what it would be and prepared to meet any surprise – First it ended at this Hou{s}e at Islington: on parting from which I pressed to attend her home. She consented and then again my thoughts were at work what it might lead to, tho' now they had received a sort of genteel hint from the Boarding School. Our Walk ended in 34 Gloucester Street Queen Square – not exactly so for we went up stairs into her sitting

room – a very tasty sort of place with Books, Pictures a bronze
statue of Buonaparte, Music, aeolian Harp; a Parrot and a Linnet –
A Case of choice Liquers &c &c &c. she behaved in the kindest
manner – made me take home a Grouse for Tom's dinner – Asked
for my address for the purpose of sending more game – As I had
warmed with her before and kissed her – I though[t] it would be living backwards not to do so again – she had a better taste: she perceived how much a thing of course it was and shrunk from it – not
in a prudish way but in as I say good taste – She cont[r]ived to dis-
appoint me in a way which made me feel more pleasure than a simple kiss could do – she said I should please her much more if I would
only press her hand and go away. Whether she was in a different dis-
position when I saw her before – or whether I have in fancy wrong'd
her I cannot tell – I expect to pass some pleasant hours with her now
and then: in which I feel I shall be of service to her in matters of
knowledge and taste: if I can I will – I have no libidinous thought
about her – she and your George are the only women à peu près de
mon age whom I would be content to know for their mind and
friendship alone – I shall in a short time write you as far as I know
how I intend to pass my Life   (*Letters*, I, 402–3)

This encounter provides an interesting comparison with his response
to the Charmian figure introduced to him at the Reynoldses. There
he resented the audience of the sisters watching for his reaction,
although, as we saw, he was quite willing to articulate and elaborate
on his response in a letter to his brother George and his sister-in-law
Georgiana. Here the episode takes on a narrative identity and a
degree of suspense as Keats engages his readers. He begins with a
walk through the streets of London which, added to the sexual alertness of the commentary, pushes the text towards the streetwalker
category. The reader is left to guess and to anticipate the sexual conclusion of the narrative. The novelistic detailing of Isabella's room
points to her intellectual independence. The bust of Napoleon, reminiscent of Hazlitt's *Liber Amoris*, probably marks her out as a liberal, while the caged birds might well signify her exotic femininity.
What Keats puts the reader through is a radical discontinuity
between a knowing expectation leading to sexual arousal culminat-
ing in an ambiguous disappointment as Isabella's rejection of his kiss
is replaced by a sensuous squeeze of the hand. Keats's own gloss on
this encounter then pushes Isabella into another category which
claims to be removed altogether from sexual desire.

The terms in which Keats removes her from the realm of his
desire is, I think, the most disturbing aspect of the letter, especially

since the narrative asks us to read the supposed Platonic, merely intellectual, category as a compensatory one brought on by the need for a post hoc justification after disappointment. And the terms of the protestation that there are only two women of his own age whom he would value solely for their minds, serve to highlight rather than diminish the extremity of his libidinised sense of the world at this point. To place his sister-in-law in that same position might also be said to lead to an embarrassing degree of ambivalence, especially since she and his brother are the recipients of the letter. Keats's reassuring claim that he is not likely to cause them embarrassment from the romantic entanglements he might be engaged in, is uneasily resolved.

At one level, the letter is a lively attempt to curtail any anxiety the recipients might have about his romantic and matrimonial engagements, but, typically, it soon develops into a profession on Keats's part as to the sincerity of his chosen vocation of poetry, his dedication to which, he confidently informs his readers, rules out the very possibility of such distracting entanglements:

> [...] These things [about existing in the realm of poetry] combined with the opinion I have of the generallity of women – who appear to me as children to whom I would rather give a Sugar Plum than my time, form a barrier against Matrimony which I rejoice in. [...] You see therre is nothing spleenical in all this. The only thing that can ever affect me personally for more than one short passing day, is any doubt about my powers for poetry (*Letters*, I, 404)

Keats's unease with women clearly goes beyond the gauche, occasionally aggressive and embarrassed self-questioning antics of a typical lower-middle-class adolescent male. There's a very particular historical sense attached to his idea of woman as a category. As we saw in his frustrated and disappointed reaction to the men of Devon and his castigation of the Scottish Kirk, Keats bemoans his contemporary society. Even more than that: he is not at home in his contemporaneity. Some of the most famous passages of his letters present this to us in graphic terms: the figure of the poet in a room with other people, but not fully present to them or himself. In his attitude to women he is similarly split between present and past, the fleeting and the eternal. Women feature strongly in this acute unease of a self in history because, for Keats, they are synonymous with the problem. For him, they are creatures of fashion and style, capable of trapping him in their enervating present.

This conjunction of women, fashion, and Keats's unease with his contemporaneity is crystallised in a letter to the George Keatses of December 1818 where he questions his brother about Fielding and Hogarth and whether they appear to him as contemporary or not. Keats then prides himself on the power of his historical imagination:

> [...] no Man can live but in one society at a time – his enjoyment in the different states of human society must depend upon the Powers of his Mind – that is you can imagine a roman triumph, or an olympic game as well as I can. We with our bodily eyes see but the fashion and Manners of one country for one age – and then we die – Now to me manners and customs long since passed whether among the Babylonians or the Bactrians are as real, or eveven more real than those among which I now live – My thoughts have turned lately this way – The more we know the more inadequacy we discover in the world to satisfy us – this is an old observation; but I have made up my Mind never to take any thing for granted [...] Perhaps a superior being may look upon Shakspeare in the same light – is it possible? No – This same inadequacy is discovered (forgive me little George you know I don't mean to put you in the mess) in Women with few exceptions – the Dress Maker, the blue Stocking and the most charming sentimentalist differ but in a Slight degree, and are equally smokeable – But I'll go no further – [...]   (*Letters*, II, 18–19)

Keats here places the historical imagination over what he terms 'our bodily eyes' or our inevitably limited contemporary perspective and suggests that he has dedicated himself to a rigorous, almost philosophical, form of scepticism. The prevailing sense of disappointment is then applied to women in general, even though, as he acknowledges in the parenthesis, his sister-in-law – Georgiana or 'little George' – is presumed to be a reader of his letter. Women, clearly, are creatures who peculiarly inhabit and are symptomatic of the present. They are, one assumes, incapable of the transcendent act of historical imagination necessary to make what he elsewhere calls 'a Man of Achievement'.

This does not mean, however, that Keats wishes only to live in imagination. His couching of our view of the present as 'bodily' clearly indicates the presence, even the prioritising, of a physical or corporeal existence. And this is confirmed later in the same letter when his noble historical scepticism leads not to a profession of cybaritic self-denial, but a rather ruthless pursuit of beauty:

> I never intend here after to spend any time with Ladies unless they are handsome – you lose time to no purpose – For that reason I shall

beg leave to decline going again to Redall's or Butlers or any Squad
where a fine feature cannot be mustered among them all [...] let my
eyes be fed or I'll never go out to dinner any where [...]

(Letters, II, 20)

Here Keats's 'bodily eye', a phrase used to describe the present,
returns with a vengeance, the present being a calculatedly intense
and urgent visual feasting upon beautiful women. As he often does,
Keats inhabits both sides of the real/ethereal dichotomy he has created, even plumping with relish for the most intense and sensational experience of the bodily present he can manage to provide
himself with.

Given this association between women and a limited, fashionable contemporaneity, those of Keats's letters which explore his
first encounters with Fanny Brawne become even more interesting.
In these, Keats playfully presents himself as investing in the workings of fashion and style. If any evidence were needed of his tendency to use letters as a means of trying out identities – even ones
which clash with his projected higher ideals of art and history –
these provide it. There's a very strong sense of the letter as experiment, a place where one can role-play, test out identities and the
response of others to them, in an intimate and dynamic environment. This has a strong visual element to it, an almost theatrical
parading of oneself in character:

Mrs Brawne who took Brown's house for the Summer, still resides in
Hampstead – she is <her> a very nice woman – and her daughter
senior is {I t}hink beautiful and elegant, graceful, silly, fashionable
and strange we {h}ave a li{ttle} tiff now and then – [...] I find by a
sidelong report from your Mother that I am to be invited to M^{rs}
Millar's birthday dance – Shall I dance with Miss Waldegrave? Eh! I
shall be obliged to shirk a good many there – I s{hall} be the only
Dandy there – and indeed I merely comply with the invitation that
the party may no[t] be entirely destitute of a specimen of that Race.
I shall appear in a complete dress of purple Hat and all – with a list
{of} the beauties I have conquered embroidered round my Calv{es.}

(Letters, II, 8)

Keats here even goes as far as seeing himself ironically fulfilling the
role of dandy, a figure for whom he often has nothing more than
scorn and ridicule. Fanny Brawne's particular connection with
fashion triggers Keats's somewhat ambivalent and mocking adop-
tion of the role, but it is one which allows him to explore his own
complex and developing response to this intriguing young woman.

The introductory comment 'her daughter senior is I think beautiful and elegant, graceful, silly, fashionable and strange' immediately registers a mixed response which, added to the revelation that they have 'a little tiff now and then', is indicative of a tension and conflict which can easily be read as desire.

Confirmation of this is provided by Keats's next in-depth account of Fanny. The letter form provides him with an opportunity of presenting her to the gaze of his recipients as well as his own. This is highly self-conscious epistolary portrait painting in which the libidinised desire signals itself precisely in the negative terms in which the portrait is couched:

> [...] Shall I give you Miss Brawn? She is about my height – with a fine style of countenance of the lengthen'd sort – she wants senti-ment in every feature – she manages to make her hair look well – her nostrills are fine – though a little painful – he[r] mouth is bad and good – he[r] Profil is better than her full-face which indeed is not full put pale and thin without showing any bone – Her shape is very graceful and so are her movements – her Arms are good her hands badish – her feet tolerable – she is not seventeen – but she is igno-rant – monstrous in her behaviour flying out in all directions, call-ing people such names – that I was forced lately to make use of the term *Minx* – this is I think no[t] from any innate vice but from a pen-chant she has for acting stylishly. I am however tired of such style and shall decline any more of it [...]   (*Letters*, II, 13)

The conflict here is telling as Keats moves through a ruthlessly exacting assessment of her physical attributes before the devastating comments about her behaviour. His admission of being 'forced' to use the term 'Minx' suggests a mock coyness on his part, given that the word could mean either simply a pert, flirtatious young woman or a wanton, lewd one. The concluding comments about 'style' and his castigation of it fit entirely with his earlier commentaries on women in relation to fashion, but just as he casts himself in the role of dandy, he is happy to experiment with Fanny in the role of a 'Minx' and to indulge himself in an overdetermined piece of conflict and supposed renunciation. That he would not 'decline any more of it' is probably very apparent from this letter alone. This is not to say, of course, that Keats's relationship with Fanny Brawne was not, throughout, characterised by a major conflict of interests between Keats's ambitions for himself as a poet and what he conceived of as the competing claims of romantic happiness. It certainly was. Their relationship is famously clouded by his assumption of the incompatibility of the two and his confirmed view that his poetic energies and power would be sapped by romance and sexuality.

In these letters Keats invokes the real and the ideal – or, to use his term, the 'etherial' – in order to explore his encounters with women. The effect is deeply ambivalent. The presence of the two categories allows him to flip between them in his representation and anxious response to women. He is able to transform the Reynolds's cousin into a Charmian, an aestheticised exotic specimen of femininity supposedly removed from the embarrassment of sexuality. As he reassures his brother that he is unlikely to cause him any trouble in the area of romance, the letter informs against him by suggesting that it is not that easy to escape sexuality. Most would agree that his encounter with this 'leopardess' is charged with desire; much more so than the Reynolds sisters themselves. A case could be made out that the category of 'real' woman Keats invokes on her behalf establishes a clear ground of sexuality on which she can be understood; and that Keats is happier in this realm of desire than he is with the stifling social etiquette, gossip, and coquettishness of the other women present in the drawing-room.

As with his commentary on the negative influence of the Scottish Kirk on social and sexual morality, Keats's embarrassment, creative as it is in many aspects, might be seen here as a product of a repressed and, to some degree, hypocritical polite middle-class culture. The letter form itself, as I've indicated, furthers this sense of ambivalence, particularly when, as in the encounter with Isabella Jones, it is mixed with a quasi-novelistic manipulation of the reader through narrative suspense. On such occasions, the reassurances to the recipient of the letter only serve to highlight the problem, the episode setting off a sexual dynamic which can't quite be contained by the confirmation of brotherly love at its end. The impression one gets is of a creative teasing out of possibilities, Keats testing out his targeted audience as well as himself. It's as if Keats plays out an, at times, almost theatrical hypothesising of himself, a daring parading of himself before his brother, which the usual pieties of letter-writing can barely contain. The peculiar closure of these texts, often, as we have seen, in the form of reassuring commitments to brotherly or fraternal affection, are seriously challenged by the combination of speculation and self-revelation on offer.

In many ways, Rousseau might have been thought of as a model for Keats's experimental letter-writing. Keats owned a copy of

Rousseau's *Nouvelle Héloïse* and even had a copy of the French writer's correspondence to hand when writing to Fanny Brawne in February 1820. His close friend Hazlitt often carried a copy of the *Nouvelle Héloïse* in his pocket, perhaps to confirm his identity as a man of radical sensibility. As a fellow liberal, Rousseau's politics might have been thought congenial to Keats while the example of his confessional writings (which have been seen as inaugurating a tradition of liberal autobiography)[5] might be thought of as offering a valuable historical example for his own exploration of subjectivity. In a relatively short letter to Fanny Brawne dated 27 February 1820, however, Keats reveals a decidedly ambivalent response to the French writer.

In this letter, Keats invokes the literary authority of Rousseau only to reject it from a position which combines a stark awareness of class difference with a familiar patriotic subscription to 'England's' masculine identity. The mobility of thought in the letter is, typically, generated by a sense of being looked at, first by Rousseau, then his 'Ladies'. What appears to be a possible quailing in the face of literary authority shifts with the emphasis on 'ladies and gentlemen' and its differentiating awareness of social rank. The next reflex is an aggressive assertion of English genius in the figure of Shakespeare. And, as if to firmly fix his own position in the middle rank of society, Keats carefully alludes to 'the common gossiping of washerwomen', assuring his reader through his use of 'must be' that he is distant from such stuff. What might have been a modest location of himself in the history of letter-writing turns out to be a robust and disgusted denial of its relevance. His patriotic rejection of what he seems to see as the false sophistication of French letter-writing and its association with aristocratic romance is followed by a confirmation of English plain truthfulness. In comparison, what he and Fanny have is love unmediated by epistolary artifice. It is plain and true, according to the national character. What might seem like an aggressively anti-literary letter is also, of course, itself highly stylised, both in its literariness – its appeal to Shakespeare and its possible referencing of Wordsworth's recent sonnet on the 'Great Men' of England – and in its own rhetorical persuasiveness as a love letter to Fanny. Its claim to true love, forcibly registered in Keats's signing off 'Good bye, my love, my dear love, my beauty – / love me for ever J-K-', is defined against what it sees as a false 'sentimentaliz'd' French form of romance.

A letter which uses Rousseau to write from the heart to Fanny Brawne provides a suitable end to our examination of Keats's extraordinary correspondence. It nicely exemplifies the complex mixture of the literary and the anti-literary which often characterises these texts. In its mercurial movement of mind and the mobility of its thought, it captures their unique flexibility. It also demonstrates Keats's tendency to imagine not only the response of his reader – that acute sense of a recipient's response with which we began this chapter – but also the degree to which letters offer him a different and distinctive set of possibilities for self-fashioning. Typically, this letter moves straight from reassuring news on the progress of his illness to the idea of being looked at by Rousseau and his ladies, only to move even more quickly to the idea of being looked at by Shakespeare. Keats has one eye on posterity, another on Fanny Brawne. Vigorous as he is in refusing the Rousseavian precedent of letter-writing and establishing himself within a gendered national literary identity, Keats nevertheless incorporates the literary into his most intimate form of writing, so that, in effect, he and Fanny are being watched by the eye of history. Constituting the heart of this very moving love-letter is the idea of being spectated, something, as we have seen, which is as important as self-presentation or role-playing in the complex representation of the self which constitutes Keats's letters:

> I have been turning over two volumes of Letters written between Rosseau and two Ladies in the perplexed strain of mingled finesse and sentiment in which the Ladies and gentlemen of those days were so clever, and which is still prevalent among Ladies of this Country who live in a state of resoning romance. The Likeness however only extends to the mannerisms not to the dexterity. What would Rousseau have said at seeing our little correspondence! What would his Ladies have said! I don't care much – I would sooner have Shakspeare's opinion about the matter. The common gossiping of washerwomen must be less disgusting than the continual and eternal fence and attack of Rousseau and these sublime Petticoats. One calls herself Clara and her friend Julia two of Rosseau's Heroines – they all the same time christen poor Jean Jacques St Preux – who is the pure cavalier of his famous novel. Thank God I am born in England with our own great Men before my eyes – Thank god that you are fair and can love me without being Letter-written and sentimentaliz'd into it – [...]   (*Letters*, II, 266–7)

Conclusion

The last manifestation of Keats's creativity in the field of love poetry is to be found in the six poems which have often been associated with Fanny Brawne: the sonnets 'The day is gone, and all its sweets are gone!', 'I cry your mercy, pity, love – ay, love!', and 'Bright star! Would I were as steadfast as thou art'; 'To Fanny' and the 'Ode to Fanny'; and the enigmatic fragment 'This living hand, now warm and capable'.[1] It seems appropriate to end this book with a consideration of this cluster of short love poems because, for a variety of reasons, they have provided Keats's readers with a difficult challenge. In these poems, Keats certainly writes out of a particularly anguished personal situation which has made for painful reading. The distressing circumstances of his illness and the precarious nature of his betrothal to Fanny Brawne can make the poems seem irredeemably attached to the private anguish of this very moving period of his life. The pressure to read biographically is greater than ever. And the fact that the poems articulate the sometimes aggressive and ungenerous frustrations of a young man in tragic circumstances has, understandably, only added to the sense of critical unease.[2] Here Keats's acute sense of bodily presence finds itself combined with physical incapacity and sexual jealousy. In many respects, however, these difficult, not always successful poems, demonstrate many of the preoccupations and creative possibilities of the earlier work. In terms of their exploration of the paradoxical tensions of passion and even in their propensity to explore the aggressive longings of sexual desire, these late poems are consistent with the rest of Keats's creative achievement.

In the first of these Shakespearean sonnets – 'The day is gone and all its sweets are gone!' – Keats takes this sense of presence, in particular the presence of the desired body of his beloved, as his

146

starting-point for a sonnet which broods, somewhat unconvincingly, on the way in which his enforced absence from her body might be overcome. Leaving behind her '[s]weet voice, sweet lips, soft hand, and softer breast' the poem contemplates the nature of this loss through its use of 'faded' as the lead word in each line of the second quatrain. As it draws to its conclusion, it registers the frustrated irony that the beloved has '[v]anished unseasonably at shut of eve': the very time at which lovers might experience 'hid delight'. The couplet which brings the sonnet to its close – 'But, as I've read love's missal through today / He'll let me sleep, seeing I fast and pray' – captures the paradox of thwarted desire in the language of the religion of love familiar from 'The Eve of St Agnes'. (Once again Keats figures himself as priest – or at least initiate – in the religion of love.) But we are left with the distinct impression that such devoted fasting is no compensation for physical presence. And the poem makes out no case for imagination as the faculty which might transcend absence or loss and compensate for the lack of immediacy provided by the senses.

The sonnet 'I cry your mercy, pity, love – ay, love!' similarly explores the nature of longing as it is focused on the body of the beloved, though here her body itself shifts between the merely physical and the spiritual as the poem expresses the poet's desire for complete possession of the other:

> O! let me have thee whole – all, all, be mine!
>   That shape, that fairness, that sweet minor zest
> Of love, your kiss – those hands, those eyes divine,
>   That warm, white, lucent, million-pleasured breast –
> Yourself – your soul – in pity give me all
>   Without no atom's atom or I die;
>
> (ll. 5–10)

In the last two quoted lines we move from a consideration of the 'soul' to a peculiarly scientific take on the body as physical object. The male self engaged in such agitated possessive longing is seen as being possessed or in 'thrall' to the enchantment of love, and the poem ends with an abrupt shift in the concluding couplet to 'Life's purposes' in which the poet reflects on 'the palate of [his] mind / Losing its gust, and [his] ambition blind!' Being possessed by desire once again leads to the spectre of the ruined masculine self – in terms of both mental appetite and ambition.

In the third of this group of sonnets, Keats takes up this idea of an abstracted steadfastness which stands aloof from the agonised changeability of human passion. Unlike the poet in his current romantic predicament, the star exists in 'lone splendour' and is able to carry out its 'priestlike task / Of pure ablution'. The proposition of the poem's opening line – 'Bright star! Would I were steadfast as thou art –' is then suddenly fractured in the sonnet's volte-face or turn at the opening of line 9: 'No – yet still steadfast, still unchangeable'. Instead of 'lone splendour', we now find the poet 'Pillowed upon my fair love's ripening breast'. The transition to the scene of earthly passion brings with it, inevitably for Keats, the 'wakeful anguish' of the human heart. In conjuring this frozen moment of passion he defines it as 'Awake for ever in a sweet unrest'. This agonised transition is then trumped even more precariously with the break in the last line of the concluding couplet: 'And so live ever – or else swoon to death.'

The threat of his own death features all too disconcertingly in 'Ode to Fanny', in many ways the most disturbing of these late poems. The ode begins with a classically disposed image of self-sacrifice, the poet offering himself up in the fashion of a priestess at the Delphic oracle:

> Physician Nature! Let my spirit blood!
>   O ease my heart of verse and let me rest;
> Throw me upon thy tripod till the flood
>   Of stifling numbers ebbs from my full breast.
> A theme! a theme! Great Nature! give a theme;
>   Let me begin my dream.
> I come – I see, as thou standest there,
> Beckon me out into the wintry air.
>
> (ll. 1–8)

This powerfully captures the combined, if conflicted, relationship between poetic ambition and romantic love. The search for inspiration is indistinguishable from his agitated 'heart' and 'breast' and the answer to his supplication arrives in the form of a vision of Fanny standing outside in 'the wintry air'. There's a chilling suggestion of death here. Keats plays with an inversion of the living and the dead (or dying) reminiscent of 'The Eve of St Agnes' where, by the end, the lovers have become spectral figures. This apparent answer to his poetic prayers turns out, in subsequent stanzas, somewhat predictably, to be the 'home' of all his 'fears' and 'panting miseries' rather than a solution to his predicament. This vision, as stanza two makes clear in the description of the poet's 'ravished, aching, vassal eyes', is symptomatic of his soul's possession by 'Love' rather than the easeful release he asked from 'Nature'.

In the next four stanzas, the attention shifts decisively from the poet's vision of Fanny to that of Fanny viewed by others, and the ode's premise of self-sacrifice switches from a logic of self-abnegation to one of self-lacerating jealousy and the misery of self-presence. Even the poem's articulation of the problem in the penultimate stanza – its own self-diagnosis of 'torturing jealousy' – provides no release. Woman's assumed fickleness gnaws at Keats's mind along with his sexual possessiveness until the poem culminates in a stanza which turns self-abnegation into a threat by proffering his own death as the consequence of any infidelity on her part:

> Ah! If you prize my subdued soul above
>   The poor, the fading, brief, pride of an hour,
> Let none profane my Holy See of Love,
>   Or with a rude hand break
>   The sacramental cake;
> Let none else touch the just new-budded flower;
>   If not – may my eyes close,
>   Love! on their last repose.
>
>   (ll. 49–56)

In 'To Fanny' the presence of his beloved is also the anguished subject of the poem against which the self of the poet is to be defined, but here, at least, other attendant worries are brought into the equation. This in some ways despairing ode begins with the intriguing idea that 'Touch has a memory', but this memory itself is seen as constituting a threat to the personal liberty and autonomy of the poet. As such, it must be 'killed'. The degree to which he is attached to the presence of his newly-defined lover contrasts markedly with what he refers to as his 'old liberty' – his former freedom to rove among the temporary attachments and distractions of female beauty: 'When, every fair one that I saw was fair, / Enough to catch me in but half a snare / Not keep me there.' In the last phase of this first section of the poem Keats reminds himself of the wilful power of such autonomy, captured in an image of an '[u]nintellectual, yet divine' seabird/philosopher '[w]inging along where the great water throes'. The figure is one of isolated heroic individuation in the face of the power of nature.

As the poem moves into its next phase of thought, it turns aggressively on love in its attempt to conjure male poetic authority from its perception of its own loss and diminution under the pressure of romance:

> How shall I do
> To get anew
> Those moulted feathers, and so mount once more
> Above, above
> The reach of fluttering Love
> And make him cower lowly while I soar?
>
> (ll. 18–23)

Conjuring the power of poetic selfhood in this way leads only to further anxiety, however. Leaving love cowering below serves only to admit another cause for anxiety: the predicament of his 'friends' – here usually taken to be his brother George and his wife Georgiana suffering financial ruin in the United States.

This America of Keats's anxious imagination is a realm of vast unyielding nature unsusceptible to culture whether at a level of animal husbandry or, more pertinently for Keats, the literary culture of European classical mythology. It is represented as a monstrous other which stands in sublime opposition to his own poetic concerns and ambitions:

> that most hateful land,
> Dungeoner of my friends, that wicked strand
> Where they were wrecked and live a wreckèd life;
> That monstrous region, whose dull rivers pour,
> Ever from their sordid urns into the shore,
> Unowned of any weedy-hairèd gods;
> Whose winds, all zephyrless, hold scourging rods,
> Iced in the great lakes, to afflict mankind;
> Whose rank-grown forests, frosted, black, and blind,
> Would fright a Dryad; whose harsh herbaged meads
> Make lean and lank the starved ox while he feeds;
> There bad flowers have no scent, birds no sweet song,
> And great unerring Nature once seems wrong.
>
> (ll. 31–43)

As if in perverse defiance of creativity, the rivers of the continent are merely 'dull', not the springs or sources of the muses; urns, equally, are unassociated with divine identity. Origins are here blank rather than inspirationally possessed. This vision of America as the inversion of nature conducive to productive creativity and as alien to mythology and history is strikingly reminiscent of the alienated and alienating landscape surrounding the knight-at-arms in 'La Belle Dame sans Merci'. There it asked to be read as symptom of the destructive potential of bewitching femininity; here it stands in displaced proximity to the agony of romance. Questions of creativity are indirectly projected onto a negative vision of nature gone wrong.

The last section of the poem – an invocation of the restorative power to be had by gazing upon his beloved Fanny – rewrites the uncanny, destructive spell of 'La Belle Dame' as natural sunny brightness to set against the dark, uncreative 'hell' of aboriginal America:

> with the new dawning light
> Steps forth my lady bright!
> O, let me once more rest
> My soul upon that dazzling breast!
> Let once again these aching arms be placed,
> The tender gaolers of thy waist!
> And let me feel that warm breath here and there
> To spread a rapture in my very hair –
> O, the sweetness of the pain!
>
> (ll. 46–54)

The last two lines capture the disturbing possession of passion to the point of Lamia's demonic energy. Even this precarious imagining of Fanny's presence is haunted by the ambivalence of his characteristic combination of pleasure and pain, perplexed as it is by the anxieties of fraternal friendship. The final twist of the poem arrives with its seemingly firm command which cuts short the invocation of presence at the prospect of the kiss. Even at the moment of imagined physical consummation Keats once again plays upon the troubling excess of doubleness – not with the 'happy, happy' of 'Ode on a Grecian Urn', but with the repetition of 'Enough!', as if to limit the excess of mere presence: 'Give me those lips again! / Enough! Enough! It is enough for me / To dream of thee!' (ll. 55–7). In this relatively short poem, the fraught triangulation between romance, friendship, and Keats's vocation as a poet which we have been following throughout this book are once again brought abruptly and jarringly together.

Although its status as Keats's last poem has now been convincingly disputed, the enigmatic fragment 'This living hand, now warm and capable' provides a suitable ending to our brief consideration of the small group of late poems associated with Fanny Brawne. In this poem, Keats's agonised sense of presence – both his own and that of his beloved – takes a new twist. Its convenient openness has, understandably, been interpreted as a moving farewell which clinches the poet's sense of his imminent death and the possibility of his fame reaching to posterity. Read as a love poem rather than as a fragment from a drama, it demonstrates the provocative mixture of pain and pleasure, aggression and sentiment which characterises much of Keats's ambivalent form of romance. Like the 'Eve of St Agnes' and other poems, it exploits a juxtaposition between corporeality and metaphysics, passion and death. The poem turns what might in other circumstances appear to be a self-abnegating gesture of love – sacrificing oneself in order to bring back a dead lover – into a palpable threat. In keeping with this group of poems, presence here is not only troubling, but aggressively haunting:

> This living hand, now warm and capable
> Of earnest grasping, would, if it were cold
> And in the icy silence of the tomb,
> So haunt thy days and chill thy dreaming nights
> That thou wouldst wish thine own heart dry of blood
> So in my veins red life might stream again,
> And thou be conscience-calmed – see here it is –
> I hold it towards you.

Throughout this book I've offered an examination of Keats's exploration of gendered identity and its anxious relationship with his poetic ambitions which often makes for uncomfortable reading. Some of that discomfort reflects the poet's own unease at his inability to resolve – or simply live with – the conflicting drives within his passionate and creative personality. As we have seen, Keats experiences a certain amount of anxiety as a result of his daring and experimental searching out of new and unorthodox modes of identity which radically challenge the strictures of the prevailing middle-class morality into which he was born. His ideas of the 'cameleon poet' and 'the Man of Achievement', as we saw in the last chapter, emerge from a precarious and passionate context of male friendship which seems particularly at odds with the dominant masculinity – indeed, with the very ethical foundation of identity in early nineteenth-century London.

As far as women are concerned, Keats demonstrates an even greater sense of anxiety, not least because they represent a threat – as he sees it – to his ambition as a poet. In addition, the conflict between his yearning for an idealised form of femininity and his full-blooded desire for actual women provides a fraught dynamic for much of his poetry and one which also signals his peculiarly sharp awareness of himself in history: his struggle with an uncongenial present and his agonised attempt to write himself into a wider historical narrative through literary fame. As we have seen, his love poetry is structured on this double sense – of the sensuous, passionate present and, through a historical and mythopoeic imagination, of an eternal realm of romance. Keeping that combination firmly in view has been my objective, even if, at times, that means we have had to take account of Keats's demonstration of a predatory masculinity and a view of women which, even in his own account, borders on the pathological. Nevertheless, in all its historical difference and occasional unattractiveness, Keats's developing sense of himself as a man and a poet lies at the heart of his extraordinary creativity.

Notes

CHAPTER 1: 'MODERN LOVE'

1. The association of Keats with a feminine form of masculinity remains, despite his being linked with Bob Dylan in a number of high-profile debates over the last twenty years. A recent Hyper-Text book claims to offer 'food for the thinking mind' by identifying useful quotations from 'movers and shakers' from Napoleon to John F. Kennedy and Malcolm X; W. Schneider delights in his proposition that 'Real Men Don't Quote Keats' (www.ascendant.ca/quotations/).

2. The spelling in Keats's letters is notoriously non-standard, erratic, and often creative. All quotations follow the text of the Rollins edition.

3. See *The Complete Works of William Hazlitt* (J. M. Dent and Sons: London and Toronto, 1930–1), vol. 8, pp. 248–55.

4. Hazlitt, *Complete Works*, vol. 8, p. 254.

5. See G. M. Matthews (ed.), *Keats: The Critical Heritage* (Routledge and Kegan Paul: London, 1971), p. 129.

6. *Keats: The Critical Heritage*, p. 129.

7. Ibid.

8. Margaret Homans, 'Keats Reading Women, Women Reading Keats,' *Studies in Romanticism*, 29 (Fall 1990), 341–70, 342.

9. Anne K. Mellor, *Romanticism and Gender* (Routledge: London, 1993), p. 179.

10. Philip Cox, *Gender, Genre, and the Romantic Poets* (Manchester University Press: Manchester and New York, 1996), pp. 81–106.

11. Marlon B. Ross, ' "Beyond the Fragmented Word": Keats at the Limit of Patrilinear Language', in *Out of Bounds: Male Writers and Gender(ed) Criticism*, ed. L. Claridge and E. Langland (Massachusetts University Press: Amherst , 1990), p. 111.

12. Susan J. Wolfson, 'Feminizing Keats', in *Critical Essays on John Keats*, ed. Hermione de Almeida (G. K. Hall: Boston, MA, 1990), p. 318. See also her 'Keats and the Manhood of the Poet', *European Romantic Review*, 6 (1995), 1–37 and 'Keats and Gender Criticism', in *The Persistence of Poetry: Bicentennial Essays on Keats*, ed. Robert M. Ryan and Ronald A. Sharp (University of Massachusetts Press, Amherst, 1998), pp. 88–108.

13. Wolfson, 'Feminizing Keats', p. 318.

14. Ibid., p. 324.

15. Marjorie Levinson, *Keats's Life of Allegory: the Origins of a Style* (Blackwell: Oxford and New York, 1988).

16. Levinson writes: 'We read the figure of masturbation as an image of productive self-alienation'; and 'Masturbation is not, then, a way to kill time, but to create it'. Ibid., pp. 46, 88.

17. Christopher Ricks, *Keats and Embarrassment* (Clarendon Press, Oxford, 1974).

18. Alan Bewell, 'Keats and the Realm of Flora', *Studies in Romanticism*, 31 (Spring 1992), 71–98, 71.

19. Ibid., pp. 94, 98.

20. Daniel P. Watkins, *Sexual Power in British Romantic Poetry* (University of Florida Press: Gainsville/Tallahassee/Tampa, 1996).

21. Richard Marggraf-Turley, *Keats's Boyish Imagination: The Politics of Immaturity* (Routledge: London and New York, 2004).

22. Robert Gittings, *John Keats: The Living Year* (Heinemann: London, 1954), pp. 65, 142.

23. William Hazlitt, *Complete Works*, ed. P. P. Howe (J. M. Dent: London, 1930–1), vol. 20, p. 146.

24. *Letters*, II, 8. Further references to *Letters* are in the text.

25. See Jeffrey N. Cox, *Poetry and Politics in the Cockney School: Keats, Shelley, Hunt and Their Circle* (Cambridge University Press: Cambridge, 1998), pp. 82–122. See also Nicholas Roe, *John Keats and the Culture of Dissent* (Clarendon Press: Oxford, 1997).

26. 'To J. H. Reynolds, Esq.', ll. 107–9.

27. 'Fame, like a wayward girl', ll. 1–3.

28. Ibid., ll. 12–14.

29. *The Letters of John Hamilton Reynolds*, edited with an introduction by Leonidas Jones (University of Nebraska Press: Lincoln, 1973), p. 14.

30. Robert Gittings, *John Keats* (Heinemann: London, 1968), p. 323.

CHAPTER 2: EPIC ABSTRACTION

1. For further commentary on the poems dealt with in this chapter see: Morris Dickstein, *Keats and His Poetry: A Study in Poetic Development* (University of Chicago Press: Chicago and London, 1941), pp. 53–129; Harold Bloom, *The Visionary Company* (Cornell University Press: Ithaca, NY, 1971; first published 1961); Jack Stillinger, *The Hoodwinking of Madeline*, pp. 14–30; Patricia A. Parker, *Inescapable Romance* (Princeton University Press: Engelwood Cliffs, NJ, 1979); Susan Wolfson, *The Questioning Presence: Wordsworth, Keats and the Interrogative Mode in Romantic Poetry* (Cornell University Press: Ithaca, NY, 1986); John Barnard, *John Keats* (Cambridge University Press, 1987), pp. 35–67, 129–38; Andrew Bennett, *Keats, Narrative and Audience* (Cambridge University Press: Cambridge and New York, 1994), pp. 72–81.

2. *Poems*, p. 506.

3. *Poems*, p. 505.

4. Ibid.

5. *Endymion*, I, ll. 36–7, 37–9. Further references in text as *E*.

6. See Nicholas Roe, *John Keats and the Culture of Dissent* (Clarendon Press: Oxford, 1997), pp. 202–29.

7. *Keats: The Critical Heritage*, ed. G. M. Matthews (Routledge and Kegan Paul: London 1971), pp. 91, 94.

8. Ibid., p. 94.

9. Ibid., p. 103.

10. Ibid., p. 111.

11. Ibid., p. 89.

12. *Keats: The Critical Heritage*, p. 89.

13. Ibid.

14. Ibid., p. 90.

15. *Hyperion*, I, ll. 42–4. Further references in text as *H*.

16. In the last three stanzas of 'La Belle Dame sans Merci' Keats writes of phantom-like 'death-pale' warriors and the 'the sedge wither[ing] from the lake' (ll. 38, 47).

17. *Keats: The Critical Heritage*, pp. 174–5.

18. *Fall of Hyperion*, I, ll. 145–6.

19. Ibid., I, ll. 187–90.

20. Ibid., I, ll. 199, 204.

CHAPTER 3: NARRATING ROMANCE: 'ISABELLA', 'LA BELLE DAME SANS MERCI', 'THE EVE OF ST AGNES', AND 'LAMIA'

1. For critical commentaries on Keats, narrative and romance and the poems dealt with in this chapter see: Earl Wasserman, *The Finer Tone: Keats's Major Poems* (Johns Hopkins University Press: Baltimore, 1953), pp. 97–137; Kenneth Muir (ed.), *John Keats: A Reassessment* (Liverpool University Press, 1958), pp. 39–41; Harold Bloom, *The Visionary Company* (Cornell University Press: Ithaca, NY, 1971; first published 1961), pp. 369–75; Jack Stillinger, *The Hoodwinking of Madeline and Other Essays on Keats's Poems* (University of Illinois Press: Urbana, IL, 1971); John Spencer Hill (ed.), *Keats: The Narrative Poems* (Macmillan: London, 1983); Theresa M. Kelly, 'Poetics and the Politics of Reception: Keats's "La Belle Dame sans Merci" ', *ELH*, 54 (1987), 333–62; David Simpson, *Irony and Authority in Romantic Poetry* (Macmillan: London, 1979); Robert Kern, 'Keats and the Problem of Romance' in *Critical Essays on John Keats*, ed. Hermione de Almeida (G. K. Hall: Boston, MA, 1990), pp. 68–87; Patricia A. Parker, ' "Keats" an excerpt from *Inescapable Romance*', in *Critical Essays on John Keats*, ed. Hermione de Almeida, pp. 103–28; Andrew Bennett, *Keats, Narrative, and Audience: The Posthumous Life of Writing* (Cambridge University Press: Cambridge and New York, 1994); Jack Stillinger, *Reading The Eve of St Agnes: The Multiples of Complex Literary Transaction* (Oxford University Press: New York and Oxford, 1999).

2. *Keats: The Critical Heritage*, pp. 157–8, 217–18. See also pp. 149–50, 170–2, 193–201, 217–18.

3. John Hamilton Reynolds, *The Garden of Florence and Other Poems* (John Warren, Old Bond Street: London, 1821).

4. Ibid., p. 158, p.v, 1. 8.

5. Reynolds, 'Dedication', *The Garden of Florence*, stanza 5, p. vii.

6. *Romantic Context: Significant Minor Poetry 1789–1830*, series ed. Donald Reiman (Garland Press: New York, 1978), p. ix.

7. Reynolds, 'The Ladye of Provence', p. 170.

8. See Kelvin Everest, 'Isabella in the Market-Place: Keats and Feminism', in *Keats and History*, ed. Nicholas Roe (Cambridge University Press: Cambridge, 1995), pp. 107–26.

9. See, for example, Harold Bloom, *The Visionary Company* (Doubleday and Faber: New York and London, 1961), pp. 375–8; W. J. Bate, *John Keats* (Harvard University Press and Oxford University Press: Cambridge MA and London, 1963), pp. 478–81; David Perkins, *The Quest for Permanence* (Harvard University Press: Cambridge MA, 1959), pp. 259–62. For a more recent account of the gender politics

involved in such manoeuvrings, see Karen Swann, 'Harassing the Muse', in Anne K. Mellor (ed.), *Romanticism and Feminism* (Indiana University Press: Bloomington and Indianapolis, 1988), pp. 81–92.

10. See, for example, Janet Todd, *Sensibility: An Introduction* (Methuen: New York and London, 1986).

11. In his revised draft Keats had replaced this expression of erotic transcendence with a much safer and much less ecstatic coupling in which the external storm obtrudes earlier on the embracing lovers whose mingling is even accompanied by the suggestion of marriage:

> See while she speaks his arms encroaching slow
> Have zon'd her, heart to heart – loud, loud the dark winds blow.
> For on the midnight came a tempest fell.
> More sooth for that his close rejoinder flows
> Into her burning ear; – and still the spell
> Unbroken guards her in serene repose.
> With her wild dream he mingled as a rose
> Marryeth its odour to a violet.
> Still, still she dreams – louder the frost winds blows.
>
> *(Poems, p. 626)*

12. See Marjorie Levinson, *Keats's Life of Allegory: the Origins of a Style* (Blackwell: Oxford and New York, 1988), pp. 255–99.

CHAPTER 4: ENDEARING ADDRESSES: THE ODES

1. See, for example, Helen Vendler, *The Odes of John Keats* (The Belknap Press of Harvard University: Cambridge MA and London, 1983), pp. 111–52; Cleanth Brooks, *The Well Wrought Urn: Studies in the Structure of Poetry* (Methuen: London, 1968, first published 1947), pp. 124–35.

2. See, for example, Cleanth Brooks, *The Well Wrought Urn*, pp. 124–35; Jack Stillinger, *The Hoodwinking of Madeline and Other Essays on Keats's Poetry* (Urbana: University of Illinois Press, 1971), pp. 167–73; M. H. Abrams, 'Ode on a Grecian Urn', 'Viewpoints', in *Twentieth-Century Interpretations of Keats's Odes*, ed. Jack Stillinger (Prentice-Hall: Engelwood Cliffs, NJ, 1968), pp. 110–11.

3. See *Letters*, II, 102–3.

4. Robert Gittings, *John Keats* (Heinemann: London, 1968), p. 315.

5. See Robert Gittings, *John Keats:The Living Year* (Heinemann: London, 1954), pp. 143–6; Harold Bloom, *The Visionary Company* (Faber and Faber: London, 1962), pp. 410–11; W. J. Bate, *John Keats* (Harvard

University Press: Cambridge MA, and London, 1964), pp. 527–30; Helen Vendler, *The Odes of John Keats* (Harvard University Press: Cambridge MA and London, 1983), pp. 20–39. Bate writes, 'Far below the standard of the other odes [...] its value is primarily biographical' (p. 528). Working from the premise that this is 'the seminal poem for the other great odes', Vendler's excellent analysis is nevertheless haunted by the suspicion of its failure, as in her comment that; 'In some ways the poem never recovers – never wishes to recover – from its sight of that spacious and unhurried Greek procession which entirely subdues the poet to its plastic grace' (pp. 20–1).

6. See: *Letters*, II, 116.

7. John Barnard, *John Keats* (Cambridge: Cambridge University Press, 1987), p. 139.

8. William Empson, *Some Versions of Pastoral* (Chatto and Windus: London, 1935).

CHAPTER 5: CORRESPONDING SELVES: KEATS'S *LETTERS*

1. For a critical analysis of Keats's *Letters*, see Christopher Ricks, *Keats and Embarrassment* (Clarendon Press: Oxford, 1974); Susan J. Wolfson, 'Keats the Letter-writer: Epistolary Poetics', *Romanticism Past and Present*, 6 (1982), 43–61; Timothy Webb, ' "Cutting Figures": Rhetorical Strategies in Keats's Letters', in *Keats: Bicentenary Readings*, ed. Michael O'Neill (Edinburgh University Press: Edinburgh, 1997), pp. 144–69.

2. Robert Gittings, *John Keats*, p. 452.

3. See ibid., p. 65.

4. See Walter Jackson Bate, *John Keats* (Harvard University Press: Cambridge MA and London, 1964), pp. 167–8, 380–4 and Robert Gittings, *John Keats: The Living Year* (Heinemann: London 1954), pp. 25–6, 30–3, 57–63 and pp. 45–53 in his *Mask of Keats* (Heinemann: London, 1956).

5. See Gregory Dart, *Rousseau, Robespierre and English Romanticism* (Cambridge University Press: Cambridge and New York, 1999).

CONCLUSION

1. All six poems have been associated with Fanny Brawne at some point, though critical opinion would now argue against 'Bright star' and 'This

living hand' being placed in this category. The former has also been associated with Isabella Jones. See *Poems*, p. 684; Robert Gittings, *John Keats: The Living Year*, pp. 25–38.

2. In his edition of *The Selected Poetry of Keats* (Signet Classics, New York and Toronto, 1966) Paul de Man makes out a case for Keats's 'latest work' as an attack on 'much that had been held sacred in the earlier work' and as a 'spectacle of a poet thus turning against himself' (p. xxvi). In *John Keats* John Barnard takes issue with de Man and argues that 'these poems cannot be understood outside their place in Keats's biography' (p. 141).

Index

CPSIA information can be obtained
at www.ICGtesting.com
Printed in the USA
LVOW04*1425280416

485766LV00018B/222/P